GREATNESS IS IN THE COMEBACK

12 Action Steps in Discovering
Ways to Reinvent Yourself.

Alease Michelle McClenningham

ISBN-13: 978-0615646824

DEDICATION

This book is dedicated to my dad, Robert (I miss you) and my mom, Pernell, who have guided me, encouraged me, loved me and consoled me. I love you more than words can express.

CONTENTS

ACKNOWLEDGMENTS

First and foremost, I want to give praises to my Lord and Savior for without you I would be nothing.

Next... Thank you to Alex B. Jones and Charles Easley for being my biggest supporters and for all of the ideas you have given me along the way; you guys saw greatness in me before I knew it existed.

Massive thanks to everyone who signed off and covered my classes at The Art Institute of Charlotte while I was on a much needed sabbatical.

This book would have never made it to print without my editor, Meredith Nourie. Thanks for the help and positive feedback.

To my aunt, Elizabeth Ann Heffney...thanks as always for the unconditional love.

I also must thank my clients and students whose questions and more questions birthed the idea for this book. The questions kept me on my toes and continue to stimulate the life-long learner in me.

INTRODUCTION

"Am I the same girl? Yes, I am… Although I have changed."
Martha Stewart

Do you have a reinventing action plan? If not, you had better start one. Successful professionals place great importance on creating an action plan that will keep them proactive, creative and accountable. They understand how to thrive and keep up in this rapid growing environment; you must constantly reinvent the way you and others see the work you do. A reinventing action plan is all about creating a personal branding image that will resonate with a target audience. To create an authentic, effective reinventing action plan, you need to be honest with yourself about who you are, the skills you have, and what you want to accomplish.

So who needs a reinventing action plan? In this era of high unemployment, nonstop global communication, and social networking sites, your personal branding image is already being shaped, with or without your input. A reinventing action plan is for anyone who wants to do what they want, so they no longer have to do what they have to do.

Greatness is in the Comeback: 12 Action Steps in Discovering Ways to Reinvent Yourself was written to help anyone on the verge of a career transition: mid-career professionals looking to change careers, a parent trying to reenter the workplace, executives who have suddenly lost their jobs due to layoffs and professionals seeking to capitalize on their skills. I want to share with you how

I'm able to work a flexible schedule and spend my down time doing what I love- spending time with family, making art and helping other creative professionals become success stories.

My focus is to share with you the power of creating a reinventing action plan. It is an action plan that will help you develop a professional image to meet the challenges of this fast-paced world, help you stand out from your competition, and improve the places in which you live and work.

HOW TO USE THIS BOOK

Greatness is in the Comeback is divided into three parts.

In **Part 1, "Training for the Comeback,"** you will discover how to assess your professional skills while learning how to manage your time and stress levels. An effective reinvention action plan, referred to as a RAP, is only as good as your ability to communicate its intent to others.

In **Part 2, "The Main Event,"** you will learn how to take your self-assessment you developed in Part 1 and begin communicating your reinvention plan effectively and professionally via social networks.

In **Part 3, "Going For Greatness,"** you will discover how to extend your reinvention plan through various media channels online and offline.

SUPPLEMENTS

After each action step, there will be RAP (reinvention action plan) exercises. Select the action step that will have the biggest impact in creating your RAP. Move on to other RAP exercises once you feel comfortable with your progress.

When you finish this book and implement the suggested actions, it becomes impossible not to see immediate, long-term, positive results. *Greatness is in the Comeback* will positively influence you in the most vital areas of your personal and professional life. *Greatness is in the Comeback* will give you the tools to manage your own career. I guarantee it will create a resoundingly successful blueprint to move you forward with enthusiasm, insight, and results.

So what are you waiting for? Let's get started!

PART 1
TRAINING FOR
THE COME BACK

"Don't call it a comeback; I've been here for years!"
LL COOL J

A few years back, a co-worker /close friend suggested that if I ever considered a career change, I should look into becoming a business strategist. He thought my greatest strengths were thinking through situations from all perspectives and being able to communicate my ideas to different types of people. I never thought of myself as a strategist. Unbeknownst to me, my strategic planning skills would be tested. Lord knows that planning and being able to create action strategies were good skills, but who knew that a life changing situation would force me to use action planning skills on myself?

In the beginning of my career, I held the position of Fashion Department Chair at a major art and design college in Charlotte, North Carolina. In that position, I successfully developed and implemented two degree granting fashion marketing and management programs. I was able to do all of this while attending graduate school full-time, teaching two courses in the program and serving on several committees in the community. I was very happy and proud of what I had accomplished, and I never thought that anything would be different. In the spring of 2004, everything I knew and felt was right with my career would change with one short meeting.

After conducting an outstanding open house presentation to a room full of eager fashion students, the dean of the college asked me to stop by his office. When I arrived, the dean and the college president were there waiting for me. They both seemed to have stressed and concerned looks on their faces. I too was concerned-what had I done? They asked me to have a seat and started the conversation with complimenting me on the wonderful job I had done with the growing, managing and developing of the fashion program and department. They went on to discuss the important part I've played in the degree granting accreditation process for the department. Then right after the accolades, they went on to say that after the spring quarter, I would no longer be able to serve as department chair for the fashion department because my educational and work experience credentials didn't meet accreditation requirements; however, the accreditation body did allow that I remain teaching within my department.

Well, there is no need to say that I was shocked – but I was also relieved. I was shocked not because of obvious reasons, but because I had received what I had prayed for. You see, just a few days earlier, while I lay on the sofa, in a small whisper I asked God, "If you could just allow me to teach and still live comfortably, I would be eternally grateful." At the time, I thought the request was selfish and down-right outrageous but clearly my request was heard.

Although I had asked for this, it didn't initially hit me that what I had worked so hard to achieve was taken away from me without any consideration to my efforts or my feelings, until I had to clean out my corner office space. In the weeks that followed, I went through what psychologists call the seven stages of grief.

1. *Shock* - reacting to learning of the loss with numbed disbelief.
2. *Pain* - as the shock wore off, it was replaced with a feeling of hurt.
3. *Anger* – hurt and frustration gives way to anger, and I began to lay unwarranted blame for my loss on others around me.
4. *Reflection* - while my friends thought I was getting on with my life, I took the time to reflect on what I was to do next.
5. *Upward Turn* - as I started to adjust to sharing a workspace with fifteen other faculty members, my purpose became a lot clearer and more systematized.
6. *Reconstruction* - as I became more purposeful, I found myself seeking realistic solutions to taking control of my life.
7. *Acceptance* - I learned to acknowledge and deal with the reality of my situation. Acceptance didn't necessarily mean instant happiness for me, but it helped me find my way forward, and it helped me to create an action plan to take control of my life.

In the spring of 2004, my chosen career path was altered. I was known in the fashion community as the go-to person for fashion marketing and management education and resources. Now I needed a different identity- a new distinctiveness that was more suited to God's next level of planning for me. It was hard at first; nevertheless, my innate strategic planning skills for assessing the positives and negatives of a situation assisted me in developing what I call a RAP (reinventing action plan).

This was my time to use this new found opportunity to do what I wanted to do, and not what I **had** to do. My RAP included a rhythmic scheme turning my passion for working with others and creating art into something meaningful and successful. I was in training for something bigger and greater than myself.

Part 1, "Training for the Comeback," provides the building blocks for creating and understanding how a RAP can help you achieve success in your personal and professional life. You will discover who you are and how to manage the world around you. This self-discovery assessment will assist you in determining your goals for the future and how your RAP relates to those goals.

ACTION #1:
IDENTIFY YOUR INTERRUPTERS

Do you procrastinate?

I do, and sometimes I procrastinate more than I should. I've learned how to identify my distractions which were causing me to procrastinate more than I should. As you know, procrastination is a waste of time and is a major contributor to anxiety and increased stress levels.

We all waste time in some form or another, but even wasted time can be productive when you learn how to use that wasted time in a beneficial way. Everyone needs time to recharge from a busy day, but what I am saying here is that when we have wasted time, we should fill up the time with productive or pleasurable activities.

Many professionals tend to jump around from one thing to the next- some call this multi-tasking. But I call this the "shiny object syndrome." In this oversaturated world of technology, we are easily distracted by the next shiny object. To stay focused and to avoid procrastination and the "shiny object syndrome," you have to identify and evaluate the distractions around you. Once you have identified these distractions, you will then be able to evaluate what actions to eliminate and which productive activities to continue.

I'm assuming since you purchased this book, you're clearly interested in the idea of reinventing yourself; nevertheless, a RAP will require balance and focus. Therefore, the first thing that must be done is to identify the time stealers of your day. Below is a list of "13 Common Time Stealers" that create major obstacles in achieving a sense of balance and focus.

COMMON TIME STEALERS

1. Background noise –the radio, television, others talking
2. Guest Interruptions – people stopping by unannounced
3. Unscheduled Meetings – events and meetings not blocked off on your calendar
4. Tasks you should have someone else do for you – trying to do everything yourself
5. Procrastination and indecision – poor goal setting and not making clear choices
6. Acting without total information – taking action on a project without clear understanding
7. OPP (other people problems) – being deeply involved with other people's issues or problems
8. Personal crisis - family member is sick or injured
9. Inadequate knowledge – not properly trained
10. Unclear objectives and priorities – projects incomplete – no deadlines

11. Lack of planning – unorganized

12. Stress, anxiety and fatigue – not getting enough sleep or exercise; poor eating habits

13. Inability to say "No"

There are quite a few aren't there? Now that you know the possible distractions in your life, it's time to learn how to get rid of them. Let's begin with taking a few minutes to ask yourself questions about how you spend your day.

Record your responses to the following questions on a separate piece of paper:

- *When did I do my worst thinking today?*
- *When did I do my best thinking?*
- *What was on my mind today?*
- *Did I figure out the answer to a problem I have been working on or thinking about?*
- *Did I allow any negative thinking to distract me?*
- *If I had to repeat today, what would I do differently? Why?*
- *Did I do anything to further my long-term goals?*
- *Did I act in accordance with my own expressed values and beliefs?*
- *If I spend every day this way for ten years, will I have accomplished something worthy of that time?*

Evaluate the strengths and weaknesses of your responses. Continue to look at your daily activities and as time goes on, you will begin to notice patterns. The important thing here is to celebrate what you are doing well and change what you aren't.

RAP EXERCISE

Let's celebrate what you are doing well. List 5 activities you feel you are doing well at managing.

The Celebration List

1.

2.

3.

4.

5.

Now, let's look at what we need to stop doing. You may need to refer back to the "15 Common Time Stealers" list for help. Write down five activities you need to eliminate from your daily routine. Remove the repetitive and/or useless tasks that consume your time. You might not be able to quit your repetitive tasks cold turkey, but you can stop **having** to do a lot of things if you plan ahead.

The Stop Doing List

1.

2.

3.

4.

5.

ACTION #2:
SELF-MANAGEMENT

Believe it or not, the concept of time management has been in existence for more than 100 years. Unfortunately the term "time management" creates a false sense of hope in what a person is able to do. Time can't be managed; time is uncontrollable, and we can only manage ourselves and our use of **our** time.

Reinventing yourself is actually about self- management. Self-management is the ability to plan, delegate, organize, direct and control every aspect of your life. Does this sound like you? In the beginning of learning how to reinvent myself, the concept of self-management seemed so far out of my reach. I could barely keep my house clean, and delegation was out of the question for a control freak like me. But as I dove deeper into creating my RAP, I quickly learned that I could actually self-manage my life. Through the process, I was able to recognize six self -management strategies I use and you too can put into action today. The following self-management strategies below have assisted me in achieving my RAP in a more efficient and effective manner.

Self- Management Strategies

Strategy #1

Always define your goals as clearly as possible. Do you find you are not doing what you want to do just because your goals have not been set properly? One of the factors which make successful and happy people stand out in the world is their ability to work out what they want to achieve in their heads and have these ideas written into goals which they can review often. Assessing your long term goals should be a part of your daily activities and be included on your "to do" list.

Visualize the possible outcome of your goals. Seek out alternatives. Choose the better of two or more alternatives. Some goals may appear difficult when you think about it but not necessarily so difficult when put into action. The same thing is true the other way around.

Strategy #2

Analyze your use of time. Are you spending enough time on the projects which may not be urgent now but are things that you need to do to develop yourself? If you are constantly asking yourself "What can I do to make things easier for me right now?" then it is time to stop reacting to tasks which may seem urgent or pleasant to do. Many of these so called urgent/pleasant activities are essentially distractions. These distractions are not helping you reach your goals.

Write down your "to-do" items in a journal so you can keep track of your schedule. It helps to remind you of your tasks and commitments. Weekly planners help you avoid the overlapping of activities. When you have overlapping activities, choose one that is a priority and then move the other activity to another day. I will talk more about creating what I call a "workable schedule" later in this action step.

Strategy #3

Have a plan. How can you achieve your goals without a plan? It's not possible. Most people know what they want but have no plan to achieve it, except by sheer hard work. What's the point in doing hard work when you don't know how to apply it? Successful people create lists that incorporate actions that will help them achieve their yearly goals. It enables them to stay on top of priorities and enables them to remain flexible to inevitable changing priorities.

When you have to complete a certain task for the first time, it is natural for mistakes to happen; however, a first time task doesn't have to be a disaster. If there is no clear goal on how things should be done, take time to plan it out before you take action. This saves time, energy, and money.

Strategy #4

Analyze your action plan. Problems will always occur even if you plan. The value of a good plan is to identify problems early and seek out solutions immediately. Good self- management enables you to measure the progress towards your goals because "what you can measure, you can control." You must be committed to building better self- management techniques into your daily routine.

Check your schedule at the start of the day. Review it in its entirety. Pay close attention to portions of your day that may be hectic and others that may not be too frenzied. Distribute your activities evenly throughout the day. Be creative when planning your time.

For example, if you need to do the laundry and you also have to rush out to buy office supplies, perhaps what you can do is to set your washing machine to do the laundry while you step out to buy the supplies. Run errands and arrive back home when the laundry is done. You can even do the cooking at the same time by using a slow cooker. You could pick up the kids from school after running errands. All it takes is developing a workable schedule that fits a busy lifestyle like yours.

Strategy #5

Create a workable schedule. While attending graduate school and working full-time, I would arrive home drop dead tried. Overworking myself was leading me nowhere but to a stressful and unhealthy lifestyle. I needed to take time out for myself, but I didn't really know how. Even if I was given ten extra hours in a day, I still wouldn't be able to get much accomplished – I was just too tired to even rest.

When planning your RAP, again, you must commit to managing your time in a more efficient manner. The lesson that you need to learn is that the more time you spend planning your time and activities, the more time you will have for those fun activities. By setting goals, eliminating time wasters and documenting your time, you'll have extra time in the week to spend on the people and activities most important to you.

There is no denying there is truth in the saying, **"Time is money."** Nowadays, I know time is a precious commodity. Once it's gone, it cannot be recovered. The fact is that when I was busy, time flew by. On the other hand, when I was doing what I call mindless activities, time seemed to stand still. I just didn't know how to manage my time. I had no control over tomorrow or yesterday. I needed to learn how to make the most of the day that had been given to me.

To be successful at reinventing yourself, you will need to create a workable schedule that will work with how you live your daily life. A workable schedule helped me to set expectations that would assist me in managing my time. It will also help you with setting goals and managing your time. You'll find relief, even if you are studying hard and/or working long hours. A well-planned working schedule makes complex issues more manageable and leaves you plenty of time during your day/week to work on activities that bring you the most joy.

RAP EXERCISE

I create a new workable schedule every 4 months. My workable schedule includes my daily activities, work, entertainment, relaxation time, and family time. I also teach my clients how to create and implement a working schedule into their RAP. Below is an example of my workable schedule while attending post-graduate school.

	Mon	Tues	Wed	Thurs	Friday	Sat/Sun
8:00-10:00	Blogging	30 min-Work out Graduate Studies	Household task	30 min-Workout Graduate Studies	Errands Appointments	Household Task
10:00-12:00	Break	Graduate Studies	Break	Graduate Studies	Meet with Clients	Saturday: Work in Studio Sunday: Church
12:00-2:00	Lunch Preparing Class Teaching	Lunch Art Marketing	Preparing Class Teaching	Blogging	Meet with Clients	Saturday: Work in Studio Sunday: Family
2:00-4:00	Teaching		Teaching	Break	Work in Studio	Sunday: Family
4:00-6:00	Dinner Preparing Class Teaching		Dinner Preparing Class Teaching	Dinner Preparing Class Teaching	Work in Studio	Sunday: Family

As you can see, my workable schedule includes my classroom teaching hours, studio time, meetings, family time and breaks. The schedule is blocked off into 2 hour sessions because it's a lot easier to schedule workable hours around my teaching hours. I'm able to cover a great deal of information in a 2 hour class, so I strongly believe I can also accomplish a lot for myself if I work in 2 hour blocks. When you create your schedule, you don't have to work in 2 hour blocks, but I do suggest you work in at least 1 hour blocks of time. In a 1 hour block, you can at least start and complete most projects (but not in one sitting).

Use the following blank schedule to fill out your recurring activities. Later in the book, you will return to your workable schedule to complete it with activities that will assist you in achieving your RAP goals. For right now, block off times that recur daily or weekly.

	Mon	Tues	Wed	Thurs	Fri	Sat/Sun
8:00-10:00						
10:00-12:00						
12:00-2:00						
2:00-4:00						
4:00-6:00						

Note: Included in the appendix section of this book is a blank schedule that you can copy and use to create new workable schedules.

ACTION #3:
BECOME SELFISH WITH YOUR TIME

How many "have to dos" each day actually don't have to be done at all? When you're trying to reinvent your life, what you choose not to do is often as important as what you choose to do. We're all given the same twenty-four hours each day. It's easy to feel like there's not enough time to do what you really want to be doing. After all the "have to dos," there's barely any time left for the "want to dos."

Developing a RAP is an on-going planning process. Every decision you make has an effect on other planning activities. By choosing to spend your time as you do today, you're deciding not to spend time doing the other things you'd really like to be doing. To make progress toward your goals, you're going to have to be comfortable with not doing some of the things you do daily. That means you'll have to allow for some negative consequences in favor of other positive consequences. Most people are primarily consumed with minimizing all of the negative consequences of their decisions instead of maximizing the positive ones. **Your time is your time**. You have to decide how to spend it, otherwise other people's stuff will consume most of your precious time. Learn to say "NO." Learn how to be more selfish with your time.

When you actually think about your list of things you're planning to do, how many of them could be deleted without consequences? The things you don't do will free up your time for other opportunities.

Taking Control of Your Life

I've advised many career professionals who sometimes get so overwhelmed with the daily demands of living that they lose focus on why they chose their profession in the first place. They want to have it all, but many of them just don't know how to get there. What I've learned and what I teach my clients is that you have to change around the order of your priorities.

During the week, I used to spend lots of time on the phone which limited my time to get things done in my personal and professional life, so I reduced my phone time - any calls after 6:30 pm could wait until the next day. It took my family sometime to get used to this, but it all turned out okay.

I also started saying NO more often! This was the best thing I could have done. Typically, I have at least one day off during the week from teaching. Many of my family and friends would ask me to run errands for them on my day off. If I have to change my schedule in anyway, then the answer is NO! If it takes me away from "me time," then the answer is NO!

Although sometimes I'm called selfish or inconsiderate, my family and friends have quickly learned to ask or mention events well in advance. Now I can put special events or errands on my schedule. This gives me the opportunity to give my family and friends my full attention without taking away from my time.

So I say to you, allow the negative consequences to happen in favor of bigger and better things. A little selfishness might be just what you need to make a breakthrough. If you were to say yes to each person that needed something from you, you would waste valuable time that leads you nowhere.

Taking control of your life

- View your workable schedule at the beginning of the week. I do this on Sunday evenings. I evaluate every appointment on my schedule. For each appointment, I ask myself "can I skip this appointment, and what will be the consequences if I do?" Then I ask myself "can I do something else with that time?"

- Create a "stop doing list." I talked about creating a stop doing list in the previous chapter, and I still stand strong on this one. Think about all the things you do on a daily, weekly or monthly basis. Pick the activities that are not helping you make progress towards your RAP. What if you just stopped doing them today? If you can't stop doing them right now, can you create a plan to make it happen in a week or month or three months from now?

- Don't be afraid to disappoint. Here's a tough one and this is where you might be accused of being selfish. When you try to please everyone around you, it becomes an impossible task that will keep you from getting what YOU want!

- Remind yourself of the things for which you are grateful. Stressful situations and daily challenges won't seem quite as bad when you are constantly reminding yourself of the things that are right in your life. Taking just 60 seconds a day to stop and appreciate the good things that will make a huge difference in achieving your RAP and other life changing goals.

- Look for the proof instead of making assumptions. A fear of not being liked or accepted sometimes leads us to assume that we know what others are thinking, but our fears are usually not reality. If you have a fear that a friend or family member's bad mood is due to something you did, or that your co-workers are secretly gossiping about you when you turn your back, speak up and ask them. Don't waste time worrying that you did something wrong unless you have the proof that there is something to worry about.

- Restore your personal priorities. Reinventing yourself can be one of the toughest challenges you pursue in your life. In fact, sometimes it can place unexpected demands on your time and energy; it can require lots of nurturing and love; it can keep you up at night; it demands structure and discipline; it teaches us valuable lessons about ourselves, and although you'll spend many long hours working your plan, it is the most rewarding thing you can do for yourself.

Devoting time to reinventing yourself should be important to you. This is the reason you purchased this book – right? Well, you have to commit to making time to work on you and your personal brand. Stay focused on the task of creating a recognizable brand for you. Learn to be more selfish with you and your time! I did and it has been the most rewarding thing I could have ever done for myself and my professional career.

RAP EXERCISE

Now it's time to go back to your workable schedule. Block out "me time".

In my workable schedule, I call "me time" breaks. My breaks consist of getting my nails done, taking a nap, surfing the internet, chit chatting on the phone, or shopping.

Your "me time" can be any of these things – just remember it's your time and you can do whatever you wish with that time.

ACTION #4:
OUTLINING THE RAP

When making the decision to create a RAP, you have to understand that this process is a lifestyle changing experience. You must remove any conflicting intentions that you may currently have. My hopes for you are that by outlining the RAP, you will become clear of your true life's purpose.

Case in point: I wasn't always clear on what I actually wanted in my personal or professional life. I was working and making a decent living, but I was working without a purpose. I was all over the place. Not until I was forced to, did I start thinking about creating an action plan for my life.

I had somewhat of an idea that I wanted to get back into creating art, but I also really enjoyed teaching. Once I started testing out a few of my ideas, I recognized what actually brought me the most joy and notoriety to my personal and professional life. I sat down at my desk and created an action plan that would help me to reinvent my personal and professional life. Even now, as an artist, educator, speaker and entrepreneur, much of the work I do is centered on helping people move through personal issues so they can be more successful.

This is how a RAP works- it defines you, but first you must define it. To develop a RAP that looks like you, thinks like you, sounds and feels like you – you'll have to answer the 3 Ws.

- Who are you?
- Why do you do what you do?
- Why should people care?

Who are you?

The first step in your outline is figuring out "Who are you?" This is the place that every creative professional has to begin. For some of you, this is already very clear, but for others this might not be so clear. And not knowing who you are isn't ok. Please understand this: you'll never find "the greatness in the comeback" if you don't know who you are. You won't see the rewards of becoming the expert, the leader, or the cream of the crop in your niche.

Often the qualities that make you who you are come so naturally to you, that you don't even think about them. Many times we are too close to ourselves to see the qualities that stand out. If you have problems with answering the following "Who are you?" questions, then pass them to different people in your life to get their responses about you and your personality.

Who Are You? Questions
1. How are you unique?
2. What are three things that make you memorable?
3. What are your special talents?
4. What do others compliment you on?
5. What do you love talking about in your personal and professional life?

See, you actually become clearer about who you are when you are going through the process of working through your RAP. Remember your plan must consist of ideas that are uniquely you. You won't have conflicting intentions about your purpose for creating a RAP. You won't be disappointed when something doesn't work as planned- you'll be able to smile and move on to the next stage of your plan. That's the whole point of taking action. These sorts of questions can help you further refine who you are. The next step is to define *why do you do what you do?*

Why Do You Do What You Do?

Many other professionals will share similar personality traits as you. That's why it is important to identify how others may connect with you on an emotional or philosophical level. In this section of your plan, it's your responsibility to make others see you as the go-to person in your niche.

Your *why do you do what you do?* statement is not about your target audience; it's about the emotional connection you make with others. Lots of professionals will serve the same target audience as you, but your *why do you do what you do* statement is what will resonate with those you are meant to serve.

To those who know me, I'm known as "the girl you contact when you are ready to take your creative business online." This is no coincidence; I realized that being "the girl you contact when you are ready to take your creative business online" was actually my *why do I do what I do* statement. My statement is based on my passion to help creative professionals like myself understand and implement internet marketing strategies into their business plan. This statement lets others know what it's like to work with you. It says something about who you are at your core, and it's the real meaning of what you want to achieve in your RAP.

Why Do You Do What You Do? Questions
1. What is your purpose?
2. What is your vision of what you hope to achieve through your work?

Why Should People Care?

Now it's all well and good to identity who you are and the reason why you do it, but there's another variable which needs to be addressed– your target audience. You need to consider if there are others out there who can help you reach your RAP objectives and why they should even care to help you out. Let me tell you something… there are people out there who need and want your help.

The minute I started researching my target audience, I quickly understood I couldn't be one person to everyone. So, like me, you will have to learn how to examine the needs of your target audience. This is going to involve you uncovering and demonstrating the benefits of working with you. What opportunities do you offer- website design, healthy hair styling, interior decorating, image consulting – these are just a few things you may do. However, these are still only features. The core benefits of these offerings must go deeper. Your core benefits are to showcase an improvement in the quality of life for your target audience.

For example, by reading this book and participating in the RAP exercises, you will begin to experience a paradigm shift in the way you think about reinventing yourself so that you can forever create a plan that will position you above your competition. You will also begin to see an increase in your confidence level when marketing on different social media platforms. I could go on and on. *Do you see how identifying benefits allows you to touch your target audience on a much deeper and more personal and emotional level?* The more benefits you can uncover about building a relationship with you, the quicker you will form an audience who cares about what you do.

Why Should People Care? Questions
1. Who is your target audience?
2. What are the needs of your target audience?
3. What are the significant benefits your target

> **audience will experience as a result of working with you?**

In today's challenging economy, gaining the trust of others is an important part of developing a successful RAP. With mergers, layoffs, and acquisitions occurring amongst companies every day, those seeking to develop a relationship or hire you will want to trust that you will do what you say you will do. The key to outlining your RAP is to show your personality (who you are), your passion (why you do what you do) and your emotional significance (why they should care) which are all a part of building a RAP that puts you ahead of your competition.

RAP EXERCISE

Summarize the answers to your questions into a four to six sentence paragraph. First, take a few minutes to filter through your answers to the questions in this action step. Try your best to write down a short verbal explanation about who you are, your vision and why you care

You are...

_____

_____

_____

_____

Your Vision is...

_____

_____

_____

_____

Why you care ...

_____

_____

_____

_____

Now turn your short explanation into a four to six sentence concise paragraph. Once you have completed this task, you will have your reinventing story.

Your Reinventing Story

_____

_____

_____

_____

_____

_____

_____

_____

Examples of Reinventing Stories

Web & graphic designer, avid art journaler, blogger and jewelry-maker in Charlotte, NC, Kelly Rae Roberts, also "Flying Lessons" alumni write about a creative journey to live an inspired life.

Valuing education is among the highest of gifts one can give another. I'm committed to both my own and my students education. Experience in and out of the classroom is truly valuable in my students education; I add value by remaining very active in the field while teaching. I have a commitment to lifelong learning, integrity and appreciation of all things- great and small. These are three concepts I wish for all of my students to take with them beyond the classroom.

I'm here to help you make money, make a difference and be your happiest, wisest and most loving self. I often say if Oprah and Jay-Z had a love child, it would be me. That's because I'm part business strategist, part marketing maven and part spiritual ass kicker with a side of hip-hop swagger.

ACTION #5:
LEARN FROM THE BEST

Reinventing lessons from famous professionals

Famous professionals such as Tiger Woods, Martha Stewart, Mohammad Ali and of course Oprah all have one thing in common- they have a well-established RAP. But creating a reinventing action plan wasn't easy for them, nor will it be for you. Many of these famous professionals have overcome huge obstacles to get where they are today. They were fired from jobs, lost millions of dollars in a business deal gone bad, told they would never succeed and even stripped of a title.

In this action step, I will share with you how famous professionals create RAPs and how they build a reputation that stands out in the minds of others. The bottom line is a RAP is critical to your future success. A RAP may sound like just another way to package and market you; it may even seem a bit manufactured and inauthentic. By now you should know that a RAP is about establishing who you are, why you do what you do and why others should care; therefore, let's move on to discovering how other famous professionals reinvent themselves.

What famous creative professionals know and you don't

Famous professionals know that an action plan of any type is an essential step whether big or small. In fact, action plans for many professionals are overlooked as not important to the success of their careers or businesses.

A RAP is basically a branding campaign which will include content, an image and promotional material which will be used in endorsing you. Your branding image is typically used on business cards, company stationary, postcards, websites, blogs and signage. Hence, the importance of a brand must be taken very seriously and with much consideration and thought. To be straight with you, a brand makes up WHO YOU ARE, WHAT YOU DO, AND WHY YOU DO IT!

Are you following me so far? These super successful, famous professionals want others to know who they are. We surely know what they do, and we watch and buy to see why they do it. Don't you want the same? Here's the next tip...

Famous professionals have good names

Your name shouldn't be taken lightly. It is how others will come to know you, so you want to make sure you use a name that's easily pronounced or/and remembered. I've had to apply this tip when establishing a name for myself. As you may have seen from the cover of this book, my last name (McClenningham) is very long and can be very difficult to pronounce and spell. So when I started building my RAP, I decided to drop my last name and only use my first (Alease) and middle (Michelle). When it came to naming my business (Alease Michelle Studios), I used a name that included my name and passion. Choosing a name for your business or product can be quite confusing. Here are a few tips you should consider:

- Choose memorable and catchy names instead of generic ones that are difficult to register in the minds of the consumers.
- Never use names that literally describe the product, such as, "The Greeting Card Store" or "The Dress Shop." Go for more creative and specialized names.
- When possible, do not use geographical names because it limits the scope of your business. However, it can be an advantage if your product is associated with a given locale.
- Keep them short and simple so as to produce memorable names.

When others encounter you, you have only three seconds to catch their attention. If you fail to do so, then you will have lost a potential admirer. Just remember: a name is not just a name; it also represents you. And in any business, the way you represent and project your image is crucial in determining your success.

Famous professionals have signature looks

In addition to creating a unique name, designing your own distinct signature look is another effective reinventing strategy that every professional should use. Aside from the name, having a signature color or logo that represents your name reinforces the potential power that you will be remembered.

A signature look is the most important part in the creation of your image. It can be used as a trademark for you, your business and product to represent its existence and identity in your niche. If you were to do a little research on other professionals in your niche, you would notice a successful signature look is one that is able to stay in the memory of admirers for a long time. This is crucial whenever you have several other similar professionals trying to achieve the same goal. For that reason, you need to produce a signature look or logo design that will easily stand out and be recognized.

Mistakes famous professionals don't make

When famous professionals embark on new reinventing plans, what they do is dedicate their time and effort to delivering an outstanding product. Famous professionals would never skimp, fall short or neglect the following:

1. Customer Satisfaction:

The RAP is just a representation of you. Therefore, it must reflect exactly what you can bring to the others and build your name from there. If you can't deliver on what you said you would, then regardless of how strong your skills are, you'll never be able to turn your planning efforts into a successful RAP. You need to be aware of your audiences' needs yet still maintain control over the image and reputation that you want your RAP to exhibit.

2. Consistency:

One of the most effective ways to build trust with others is to be consistent with the message you are trying to convey. Consistency is most important when showcasing the values that are key and important to you. Every aspect of a professional's image must remain consistent with his/her values, vision, and representation.

3. Expanding the Brand:

Creating a RAP for you isn't limited to the creation of a signature look, logo and name. These are just statements of your professional image, but there are several factors in between that would help transport it into more awareness. In every form of communication that is sent out, include a photo or logo, social media account URL, and a tag line. Whether on a business card, newsletter, letterhead, invoice, or envelope, all branding elements are of no use unless you are able to capitalize on it and make it do its work for you.

4. Managing the Brand:

As market trends continue to change and evolve, so must reinventing strategies. When setting up a RAP, there is also a need to look into expanding your talents which is one of the most effective ways to generate more responsiveness to a personal image. When there is an opportunity for improvements, don't be afraid to act on them. Being on top of things and keeping up with changing trends in the market is a great managing strategy.

RAP EXERCISE

Creating a RAP for your professional life is never easy, but once you recognize the factors that could impede your progress, then you're on your way to a super successful reinventing image. It's important not to be fake. Make sure what you put out there is real and not just another cheap substitute of someone else's RAP. The key to building stronger, purposeful relationships is to NEVER copy others but to observe what works for others and learn how to make it your own. It's about, more or less, developing an action plan that is made **by you for you**.

The following RAP exercise is to locate and research three famous professionals in your industry. Observe and write down all online and offline marketing strategies they are using in reinventing themselves.

List the names of three famous professionals in your industry.

1. _____

2. _____

3. _____

Note what marketing strategies you like and dislike about their marketing.

Famous Professional	Like	Dislike
1.		

2.

3.

Write down 3 things you would like to use in your own reinventing plan.

1. _____

2. _____

3. _____

PART 2
THE MAIN EVENT

"The real glory is being knocked to your knees and then coming back. That's real glory. That's the essence of it." ***Vince Lombardi***

On March 8, 1971 at Madison Square Garden a defeat occurred that no one would soon forget- Muhammad Ali was dealt his first professional loss in "The Fight of the Century." After this fight, Ali would go on to lose two more fights. Then came "The Rumble in the Jungle" in October of 1974, positioning Ali against George Foreman. The odds were against Ali; no one expected the former champion, now 32 years old, to have a chance at winning. But his faith in himself helped him to overcome the odds because Ali knocked out Foreman in the eighth round to regain his title as the heavy weight champion of the world. Although I was too young to remember this fight, I do know that Muhammad Ali's story inspires me to stand tall even when the odds are against me.

After having been told that I would have to resign as department chair of the fashion department, I soon realized that an announcement of my resignation would occur at the next faculty meeting. At the time, I was in stage three (anger) of the grieving process, and I thought it would be best for me not to be present at said faculty meeting.

This faculty meeting was my main event and just like Ali, it was my time to stand strong when others thought I was defeated. Actually during that faculty meeting, I was the person who stood up and announced the news of my resignation. Although that was the hardest thing I've done, it was also the best thing I could have ever done for myself.

So I say this: You must be the greatest, you must be the driver of your destiny, and you must remember that greatness is not defined in moments of victory; it is defined in the moments after defeat. It's your life, and you only have one life to live. Decide NOW to live your life the way you want it, not the way someone says you should live it.

Now I can actually say that it's possible and I'm able to share with you how I was able to turn a devastating life changing situation into a transformative success story. A RAP requires balance, action and focus. Learning how to reinvent yourself should be a part of your daily trainings, but sometimes our lack of confidence and know-how can make the process challenging.

I knew I was on the right track because good things began to happen. In 2005, I was awarded a faculty monetary grant to purchase art supplies to produce artwork. With the money I received from the grant, I was able to produce enough artwork to showcase in my first gallery show – and 90% sold out within days of being hung. Art galleries and national media sources began to take notice of me. I was asked to exhibit my work in their galleries and the media asked for interviews and photos of my work to present in their magazines.

In my journey to reinventing myself as an artist and educator, I developed a RAP that would be accessible anywhere and to anybody seeking the next best professional. My RAP included the use of social media; it was and still is the best way to stand out amongst others. It is the most important action step in the RAP. According to a report by Nielson,

"In the U.S. alone, total minutes spent on social networking sites have increased 83 percent year-over-year. In fact, total minutes spent on Facebook increased nearly 700 percent year-over-year, growing from 1.7 billion minutes in April 2008 to 13.9 billion in April 2009, making it the No. 1 social networking site for the month." http://www.nielsen.com/us/en/insights/press-room/2009/time_on_facebook.html

Even with statistics like this, many professionals still feel that social media is a waste of time, and that it's just a place to share what you ate that day. To be honest, many people do use social media platforms to share personal and mundane events. But what will make you different than most is that you will create a RAP that will assist you in developing a social media marketing campaign that will cause you to stand out among the millions of people using social media.

Are you prepared?

Today, social media platforms have invaded and taken over our public consciousness. It has become a big part of day to day routines and a crucial communication tool for people to connect and stay in touch. Your friends, co-workers and employer have and will continue to use social media presence as an integral basis of a person's legitimacy, reliability and viability. Suffice it to say, social media has managed to steal some of the thunder away from traditional self-promotion methods.

Given the power of social media, it is critically important for you to develop processes to lead to efficiency and successful social engagement. Discover how social media can become your most effective and influential event in **Part 2, "The Main Event.**

Part 2 of this book will provide you with all of the necessary information to understand the full potential of social media, as well as how you can harness its hidden power so you can make smarter decisions on how you can effectively incorporate it into your own reinventing plan. This section will equip you with all of the action steps on how to get started and use social media to its full advantage and its long-term rewards.

ACTION # 6:
USE WHAT WORKS: SOCIAL MEDIA

Everyone I know is using social media to reinvent themselves. Are you? This is a bold and totally ridiculous statement to make, but I'm not totally wrong. A lot of professionals are using social media to reinvent themselves. As more and more professionals readily use social media platforms, there's increasingly been an acceptance and expectation for social media to promote your skills in the idea of social commerce.

Given the promising potential of social media, it is important to be flexible and adjust with the ever changing trend of promoting what you do and are good at in a technically sociable medium. By taking time to learn and use what works with other professionals, you too will be able to sustain healthy social engagement activities which will include building communities and relationships by listening, responding and creating value.

There are several social media definitions to be found, yet there's no clear definition of social media that's suitable to all situations; therefore, to make it clear for you and for the remainder of this book, I'm offering my definition of social media that I believe is best suited for a reinvention action plan:

Social media is about using online tools that promote sharing and conversation. This ultimately leads to engagement with current and future customers and influencers in your target market. Effective social media starts with an action plan that helps to position you as the expert in your niche through stimulating, informative and helpful content.

Why social media?

At this point, I'm going to make the assumption that you are willing and ready to create an action plan to reinvent yourself. If you aren't, then I think you are doing a great disservice to your professional and personal lifestyle. Social media is a great tool for marketing who you are and what you do. Social media can open up a lot of doors for you. It's a simple and effective way to build confidence in what you do and know about your passion and purpose. I honestly don't understand why anyone wouldn't want to use a tool that would clearly propel their future goals. I sort of understand if you still may think that social media sites like Facebook are for self-centered people. I thought the same thing in the beginning stages of social media networking until I realized that social media wasn't all about posting what I ate for lunch.

Social media is one of the best and most suited platforms to support a reinventing action plan. Let me share with you why social media is important:

1. Social media makes communicating with those who are interested in your talents easy and fast.
2. Social media allows you to educate your followers by providing them with links, articles, or books that have helped you with your personal and professional development.
3. Social media permits you to build a relationship with future prospects that you may not know or feel comfortable conversing with face-to-face.
4. Social media can generate a buzz about your creative talents.
5. Social media allocates a way to provide quick responses about new products or ideas you may be involved with.
6. Social media is an extension into a global market.
7. Social media provides an archival resource of your success which grants you the time to reflect on your passions and purposes.
8. Social media helps you become a better communicator and presenter of your work.

As you can see, the common attribute of social media is that it enables you to showcase who you are and what you know and are passionate about. Regardless of which platform you use - social networks, blogs, microblogs, social bookmarking sites or multimedia - the important takeaway here is to choose a platform that's best suited to your personality, skill level and schedule.

Each social media platform mentioned above can serve as a powerful tool in your RAP. Use the Social Media Chart to help you plan out which social media platform is best for your RAP goals.

The Social Media Chart

Category	Description
Social Networking	Social networking is a way to engage and interact with a specific online community by way of personal or business page. It's an effective medium for conversation with your other like- minded creative professionals; it increases your exposure through the public broadcast feed system and can tap into specific community types. Goal: To build a fan base where current and potential clients can interact in one central

	location. Examples: Facebook, LinkedIn, Google+
Blogging	Blogging is an informal conversational medium for writing and publishing content about you and your interest on a regular basis. It is a very simple medium to start with; it is a convenient way of providing useful resources to a specific audience and has the potential to share detailed information about you. Goal: To establish yourself as an expert and encourage a conversation with your target audience Platforms: Blogger, Typepad, Wordpress
Microblogging	Short –form blogging where posts are usually limited in length and format. Can grow exposure to a large group of influential online

	users in a short span of time. It's a good way of finding out news on a particular topic as it happens. Goal: You want an immediate way to interact with your consumer base Platform: Twitter, Tumblr,
Social Bookmarking	A central location for posting links to useful resources which can be seen and shared by other users. Allows quick spread of your content. Useful place to read news, insights and updates about your industry and partners. Goal: You want to share useful resources relating to your industry with your target audience. Platform: Digg, StumbleUpon, Delicious

Multimedia	Sharing rich media such as video, images, and presentations online. More engaging and interesting than text-based media. More likely to be shared than other forms of media. Compact way to communicate a large amount of information.
	Goal: Your business lends itself to how-to or viral videos or rich content such as images and presentations.
	Platforms: YouTube, Vimeo

How to harness the power of social media

Social media is a constantly evolving medium. It's no wonder many professionals struggle to figure it out and keep up with the changes. An increasing amount of professionals have enjoyed quantifiable success, but there are also many who have failed. Failure is often brought about because of not understanding how to use social media in the most effective manner.

Much like dating, to be successful and build a strong relationship with another person, you will need to woo, nurture and meet the needs of your "partner". To help you out, below are the following rules that apply to the beginner, intermediate and advanced social media user. If you seriously want to harness a powerful platform to propel your career, acquire new clients, increase your worth as well as be noticed for what you do, here are the golden rules you should abide by and respect:

Golden Rule #1: Social media is all about building relationships, not business transactions. Any attempt to overtly sell yourself can easily damage your online presence. Consumers no longer have to think of excuses and come up with a polite "no" to a persuasive self-promotion; all they have to do is click the "unfollow" button.

Golden Rule #2: You must learn and observe what works on social media sites. Don't make the mistake of just jumping onto a social media site without observing what others are doing. Look for other professionals who are engaging and have lots of followers.

Golden Rule #3: Focus on cultivating engagement and not on figures. The number of followers, likes, and the size of network should not be considered as performance indicators. There is greater value in maintaining a smaller network with regular interactions and active engagements.

Golden Rule #4: Define your target audience and identify specific area of expertise. Don't try to be all things to all people. If you are truly keen on reaching power users, key decision makers and influencers, your content should be designed around your market.

Golden Rule #5: Content is king in social media. As stated, social media is not a place to publish your award-winning sales pitches. Posts should be clear and concise, not emotional or impulsive. They should be carefully constructed and always politically correct. They should be free from any gimmicks or hidden strings attached but provide information, free resources and best practices.

Golden Rule #6: Updates should be frequent and consistent. Social media activities are long-term and ongoing efforts and work as an integral part of your online presence. It is not an 8 to 5 weekday job. It's best for status updates and posts to be published no more than 2 to 3 times daily.

Golden Rule #7: Social media profiles MUST be impeccable. Profiles are the first and most viewed page in social media platforms. But all too often, they are the most ignored aspect. All elements, including background, images and messages should be consistent.

The 6 Step Method: Creating your social media RAP
According to the Social Media Marketing Report for 2010, an estimated 67% of business professionals have actively increased

and strengthened their social media efforts. More and more professionals are seeing the importance of social media and many of them are incorporating it into their professional development. Without a plan or strategy, your presence might as well be nonexistent.

But how do you exactly develop a Social Media RAP to best cater to your personal image and to the unique characteristics of your target audience? There is a method to the madness. First, before you start formulating your social media section, it is absolutely critical for you to believe in the potential of social media and that the primary goal isn't simply to promote yourself but to build community around what you believe in and value.

You shouldn't launch a social media RAP just because everyone else is doing it. Social media is not a temporary marketing gimmick or project with an expiration date but a long-term commitment with invaluable benefits. Now that we have that covered, below are the six methods I used and now you too can use them to guide you through developing your very own social media RAP:

1. **Define your goals and objectives.** Determine what your specific social media objectives and goals are and how they

complement and support the overall goals of professional development. The most common goals include:

- Enhance presence across social media platform
- Increase traffic to personal website or blog
- Develop relationships for potential partnership opportunities in the future

2. **Research, research and more research.** Research is very important as a basis for execution. This will include choosing one social media platform that best suits your goals, technical skills and schedule. Take time to check out what's out there, and observe what others in your field are doing.

3. **Prepare a database of contacts and content.** If you go about your social media RAP correctly, social relationships will start to develop naturally. Start establishing connections by following conversations relevant to your industry. Make a list that will identify the key influencers and power players that have important roles in your industry.

4. **Join conversations to start developing and forging relationships.** Start answering questions relevant to your industry; give your opinion and join a group. This will not

only help you start your network, it will also help you build your reputation as an industry expert and a thought leader.

5. **Strengthen your social media relationships**. Don't just hide behind your profile photo; make your presence known by attending events that encourage face-to-face interactions. This includes offline events that are relevant to your industry.

6. **Analyze, measure, adjust and improve**. After about six months, it's time to measure your success and progress toward your goals. You need to analyze and identify key areas that need improvement, adapt to any changing trends and then improve your overall social media RAP to fit those changes. Remember, it's not always a straight road ahead, so you need to constantly evaluate and adjust.

RAP EXERCISE

1. What is your social media goal?

   _____

   _____

2. Choose one social media platform from each category and fill out the chart below.

Social Media Platforms	Name of platform	Likes & Dislikes	Use in social media RAP	
Social Networking			Yes	No
Blogging			Yes	No
Microblogging			Yes	No
Social Bookmarking			Yes	No
Multimedia			Yes	No

ACTION # 7:
NO ONE SIZE FITS ALL

The act of building trust in the world of social media means becoming a friend, a confidant, a problem solver and a guide to millions. When you are able to do all these things, you'll gain trust and a fan base that will adore you for many years. **It sounds simple, doesn't it?** In a way it is, but it all depends on you choosing and using the right social media communication platforms that are best suited to your personality, skill level, and time availability.

There is no one size fits all in social media. Action #7 will enable you to hit the ground running on each of the most popular social media platforms being used by professionals. Even if you already have accounts set up, I strongly encourage you to take a quick look through each social media platform mentioned in this action step. You might learn a few new tricks, or perhaps I might be able to persuade you to launch your RAP on a different platform. Either way, this section will provide you with valuable references that you can review whenever you need assistance on a particular aspect of managing your social media accounts.

Action #7 will discuss Facebook, Twitter, LinkedIn and Google+.

Facebook: A Powerful Marketing Medium

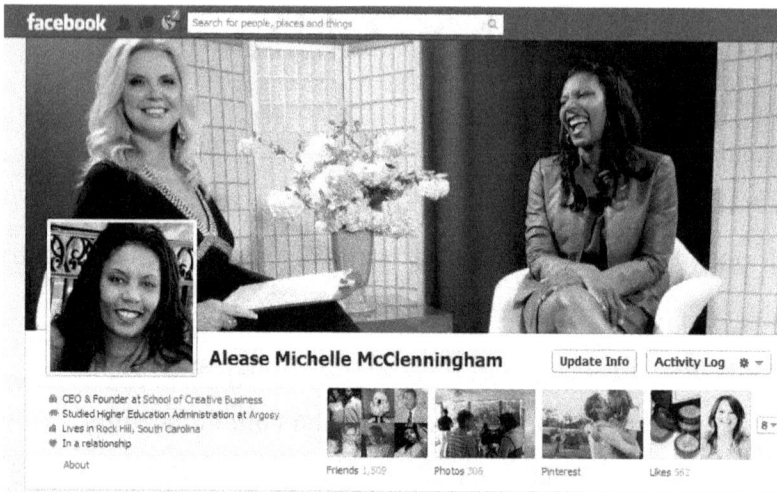

Facebook is perhaps the most famous global phenomenon that has continued to grow exponentially since its launch. Originally designed for college students, you don't need statistics to prove that Facebook has moved leaps and bounds beyond its original use. Over time, it has been recognized as an extremely powerful networking medium for professionals and businesses.

What is it?

Facebook is a type of social networking service that was launched in February 2004 and is privately owned and operated by Facebook, Inc. Recent reports as of February 2012 indicate that Facebook has reached an astonishing 845 million active users. To use its services, users need to register and create profiles; from there, members can exchange messages, post statuses, upload photos, chat with friends and so much more. It began as a simple social medium and has evolved into a widely popular professional networking site.

Why use Facebook for networking?

Creating a Facebook page provides you with a powerful tool to interact with your market on a different level that traditional media will not be able to provide. By helping your fan base gain a close connection with your personal brand, you can turn them into loyal patrons and unpaid brand ambassadors. Let's examine the many ways you can benefit from Facebook:

- **Great exposure**. With millions of users, Facebook offers unrivalled potential for exposure. When used strategically and consistently, Facebook can contribute to the significant increase in your company's online presence and visibility. Post comments, provide insights, give advice and tips to earn respect and credibility in your network and ultimately gain leverage.
- **Improve Google rank.** With Facebook's "Pages" application, you can create a professional profile to showcase your products, services and business. Within these pages, you are provided with the option to include

links to your website and "like" buttons. This helps drive traffic towards your site and generate more interest.

- **Powerful marketing platform for free.** The use of Facebook, as you may already know, is absolutely free of charge. It allows you to reach out to hundreds, even thousands of people, with a host of user-friendly applications and tools you can use to market yourself, your products and services.

- **Targeted advertising space.** For a reasonable fee, you can create ads and target them to reach a specific gender, location and age group, as well as track its performance.

- **Provide regular updates.** Facebook offers you a convenient way to update your network on general information about you and new products and promotions to stay fresh and relevant in the minds of your target market.

- **Facilitate online discussions to gain valuable inputs.** Use newsgroups and networks as a venue to discuss and respond to comments and inquiries. It is also a great source of constructive feedback to help you enhance your personal and professional image.

- **Stay connected and nurture relationships.** Provide useful information to your network on a regular basis. This includes helpful how-to videos and other relevant content which your market may enjoy.

Optimizing and Engaging

Google loves Facebook and the more you participate on the Facebook network, the more chances you have of being found by others. Here are a few tips I've learned about optimizing and engaging on a Facebook Page:

- **Add content.** Include key information such as a website link, bio, location, and photos so others will have a general idea of who you are and what you do. Focus on providing brief but engaging information in the "about me" section of your page. *Power Tip*: If you will key in your website URL starting with http:// in the info box right under the profile picture, Facebook will automatically turn it into a clickable link. This will allow you to conveniently refer visitors to your website, twitter account or personal blog.

- **Invite friends**. Invite your friends, family, and co-workers to "like" your page. You can send out an email, personal newsletter, advertise on your site, post links, or promote through flyers, etc. The efficient way to set up your Facebook page and add existing clients is to create a separate Gmail account for your Facebook account. Import the email addresses of your clients there. When you create your Facebook page, the system will automatically find your friends from your address book and suggest them to become friends on Facebook.

- **Add the "LIKE" button to your site**. To effectively promote your Facebook page, add the "like" button to your website and blog so people can engage with your page as well as share it with their own network.

- **Interact and join the conversations**. Maximize visibility and presence by posting regular updates on your wall about what you do and value. You can also provide helpful tips and quotes that will generate interest and comments and drive active engagement.

- **Build deeper relationships**. Use this opportunity to get to know your loyal fan base and go out of your way to make them feel at home by responding to comments in a timely manner.

- **Get a vanity URL.** Instead of the unappealing ""3267783386?ref=sg&ajaxpe=1&_a=7" URL, customize it into something more professional, like http://facebook.com/yourname. To be able to do this, you need to have at least twenty-five friends.

- **Customize your cover image.** To stand out, you need to have an attractive and striking cover image which can significantly help visitors become fans of you and your page. If you don't have access to photo editing skills, you can hire someone from Fiverr.com to help you out.

Tips on promoting your Facebook page

1. Use the search function:

- Actively add people that can potentially become clients or those who relate directly to your specific line of business.

- Discover relevant or related personal and business pages, events, people, and groups. This can also be used to keep track of any brand mentions as well as provide timely feedback. Communicate on your page! Facebook is about building relationships. Make sure to answer back when others leave comments. When you are composing a status update post or message, mention the person you are referencing with an @ sign.

2. Cheat a little.

Ask friends, family members and fellow co-workers to post comments and "likes" on your status updates in order to boost rankings. Status updates that have five or more comments and "likes" will show up in the "Top News" feed. This will also help make your Facebook wall more active and inspire fans to participate in conversations.

3. Fill your page with media content

- Upload photos of you doing what you do so fans can easily relate to you.
- Upload photos of events you hosted and tag your fans
- Post videos that feature you
- Use video to respond and entertain your fans

4. Keep your fans updated.

Direct messages are very powerful, but make sure not to abuse it. Before you send messages to your fans, think twice. Your updates should be valuable since your goal is to inform and engage and not irritate.

5. Build partnerships with other Facebook pages.

Each page on Facebook features a function called "Add to My Page's Favorites" button. Any "favorite" will have their profile image displayed in the "Favorite Pages" featured on your Facebook page. Also seek help from your fans in building your community using the "Suggest to Friends" and "Share" tools.

6. Use applications.

There are some really useful apps on Facebook that you can readily use to promote yourself. You can conduct polls and quizzes. There are even apps for giveaways and sweepstakes – something most fans love to participate in.

7. Spy!

Yes, you also need to keep an eye on others like you, especially those that are highly successful in their own campaigns. Check out what they are doing every now and then and study their strategies. If you choose to copy, make sure you offer the better version.

Twitter: Online Fame in 140 Characters or Less

Twitter's simple question: "What are you doing?" has certainly generated a lot of response since its launch. From teenagers to professionals, celebrities, politicians, corporate bigwigs – you name it - everyone is on Twitter. With the quick and frequent exchange of ideas, opinions, and answers, Twitter has created a whole new universe for people from different social backgrounds, statuses and interests to stay connected through a more open line of communication.

Understanding the Twitter phenomenon

What is Twitter? According to Wikipedia.org, Twitter is another popular social networking and microblogging service that allows its users to send and read text-based posts or "tweets" of up to 140 characters. Twitter was created by Jack Dorsey in March 2006 and was officially launched in July of the same year. Since then, the service has gained worldwide popularity and currently has 300 million users, generating more than 300 million tweets as well as handling more than 1.6 billion search queries every day. Twitter has been described as the "SMS (short message service) of Internet". (http://en.wikipedia.org/wiki/Twitter)

Twitter offers a combination of different forms of communication -- text, photos, music, videos –commenting on everything from everyday life experiences to interesting content, newsworthy events and crises. Conversations can revolve around hot topics using hashtags # and users can post and view updates, follow other users, as well as send public replies or private messages to connect and communicate with other users.

Why use Twitter?

Twitter can be quite annoying if you alert your friends to your actions on a regular basis, but don't rule it out as an important tool to promote your RAP. For instance, use Twitter to...

- **Connect with others**. This is the primary reason why you should make use of Twitter. Twitter has become so much a part of everyone's daily routine that it's the perfect venue on which to connect, interact, and study your target audience.

- **Promote your image.** You don't have to be in the league of Nike, Dell or Starbucks to brand and generate interest. In fact, it presents the best platform for professionals to reach their target industry.

- **Market.** With its wide reach, you can use Twitter to market what you do, your accomplishments, products and/or services to a wider market, and the best part is that it's free.

- **Share news**. Twitter is the best and fastest way to publish the latest updates about what is happening in your professional and personal life without needing to compose long, elaborate content.

- **Go viral.** Once you have managed to gain a degree of popularity, you will discover how viral it can be. This can become a strategic edge for your marketing campaigns.

- **Spy on the competition**. You don't just gain insights on customers and your target market, you can also read and study what the competition is doing, what their weaknesses are, and you can work on positioning yourself to be better.

- **Network**. Connect with industry leaders, the movers and shakers and influential personalities relevant to the industry you operate in. If you have attended networking events in the past and have enjoyed decent results, just imagine what Twitter can do for you.

- **Generate website traffic**. When done perfectly, Twitter can be a great and effective tool to generate more interest and attract targeted markets to visit your website or blog which can translate to leads and ultimately convert to job offers, speaking engagements or sales.

- **Share**. Twitter is a perfect venue to showcase your skills and expertise and provide sound advice, opinions and help resolve problems to gain more credibility as a thought leader.

How to build and attract followers

As you might have already guessed, Twitter can become an essential social media tool to drive your RAP forward. It's not your typical fly by night trend that will eventually disappear into extinction. Since its launch, it's on the upswing. To be able to take full advantage of the full potential of Twitter, you need to carefully plan out your strategies.

- **Conduct an initial search**. Create your Twitter account and use the Twitter search to check out the buzz about your name or brand, your direct competitors and other relevant words that relate to your company, products and/or services.

- **Add a photo**. It's unappealing and downright rude to interact with anyone without a photo. It is generally best to use a personal photo of yourself. If you don't have a nice photo of yourself, I strongly suggest you hire a photographer to take professional photos of you.

- **Start joining conversations and talk to people about their interests**. This will convey a more personalized appeal that will show a more authentic side of you.

- **Generate interest**. Post interesting things that relate to your industry and not just about you. Share interesting and fascinating links that will entertain and spark interest.

- **Say no to obvious marketing**. Don't make the mistake of overselling your products and/or services. Others will either tune you out or hit the "unfollow" button.

- **Become more human**. Promote interesting, outside of work stories about yourself.

- **What to Tweet about.** Ask questions and encourage your followers to share their opinions, tweet about other people instead of simply focusing on you, deliver content in the form of pictures, links to interesting articles, advice that's insightful and as a general rule of thumb, tweet at least eight times in a day and no more than fifteen times.

Twitter power tips

1. You don't have to read every single tweet.
2. You don't have to reply to every single @ tweet that has been directed at you.
3. Choose direct messaging options if exchanges with other people do not have value to other Twitter followers.
4. Regularly check out the Twitter search function to find out if there are people talking about you, your brand, company, products or services.
5. One great way to build community in Twitter is to respond to tweets as well as re-tweet other user's posts.
6. Complete your profile information.
7. Add Twitter feed to other social media profiles and blogs.
8. Reply to people who are following you, and most especially to those who don't.

Creating your Twitter account is just the start of your journey. To get the best results, Twitter, along with other social media platforms, should be ongoing projects.

LinkedIn: Build Your Network

Most professionals use LinkedIn in order to "link to someone" to form a partnership, make a sale, or get a job. Given its continuing success, it works quite well in that many professionals from consultants to CEOs and business tycoons maintain an account representing 130 different industries across the globe; however, to date, LinkedIn still remains an underutilized tool as many of its users have not fully explored its full potential nor maximized its benefits.

What is LinkedIn?

LinkedIn was launched back in 2003 and since then it has become the world's largest and most popular professional networking site. An estimated 1 million new members join this social media platform every week. People generally connect on LinkedIn with people that they personally or professionally know. However, unlike Facebook and Twitter, LinkedIn is perceived to be more business focused.

LinkedIn presents a great venue for its users to make or establish second or third-degree introductions and connections, which can be useful when looking for a job, recruiting talent or seeking other employment opportunities.

To date, LinkedIn maintains over 85 million members across more than 200 countries which include top executives from almost every Fortune 500 company.

Why use LinkedIn?

Some professionals consider LinkedIn a go-to platform for people seeking employment. It's certainly more than that. It is a great way to build a portfolio and a reputation, as well as connect with like-minded individuals to promote your brand, products or services. LinkedIn is outstanding for...

- **Increasing visibility.** By establishing connections, you also increase your exposure and visibility. Whether you offer a product or service or both, your profile may be made available to people interested in doing business with you, forging partnerships or participating in hiring services.

- **Expanding network.** Connect with people ranging from past acquaintances, people from your school, past companies, to affiliations and those who share your passions and interests.

- **Improving Google page rank**. LinkedIn allows its users to publish and make their profile information available for search engines to index. LinkedIn profiles rank high in Google, so it's a great and effective way to influence other people's perceptions when they search for you.

- **Scoping out the competition**. LinkedIn is one perfect way to keep tabs on your competition as well as on partners and customers.

- **Highlighting recommendations**. LinkedIn is more like a living, breathing resume of professionals that comes complete with recommendations from people you have worked with and worked for in the past.

Customizing your LinkedIn account

When it comes to ensuring the effectiveness of your LinkedIn page, relevance is important to establishing and maintaining strong connections. You'll want to take time to customize your LinkedIn profile for a number of reasons. Social media accounts for businesses should be created in line with the RAP purpose and goals in mind.

When creating your profile, you want to attract a particular audience. If you check out the profiles of CFOs and compare them with community managers, you will immediately recognize the difference. When customizing your LinkedIn profile, make sure to keep your target audience in mind.

Here are the areas you'll need to customize:

- **Summary.** This section should showcase your skills, assets and expertise in three to five short paragraphs. Create content that will grab attention and generate interest on the exceptional highlights of your professional career. Highlight achievements and specialties using concise words. You can use bullet points to make it more readable and drive more emphasis.

- **Professional headline.** This appears similar to the description in your "Current Position" unless you change it. This one appears below your name.

- **Add a photo.** If you have other social networking accounts, you probably don't accept connections with people who don't display their profile photos, right? The same applies with LinkedIn accounts. Make sure to choose a close up headshot photo that best represents you professionally. Remember, you are your own brand, so make sure your photo demonstrates that.

- **Experience/work history.** Since LinkedIn is a professional networking site, make sure to highlight your best and most positive work experiences. This is an opportunity to showcase your successes. While you are not limited with the number of words you can use, make sure to keep it concise so you won't lose the attention of your audience.

- **Recommendations.** Allow others to rave about your character and capabilities with recommendations or through endorsements. You have the ability to approve and manage your recommendations, so be sure to only approve the positive feedbacks. If you don't have any endorsements, you can ask someone like a colleague, client or past employer.

- **Skills.** What is it that you do that's different? Your personal skills are those that make you marketable.
- **Certifications, licenses and accreditations.** Make sure to take time and fill in this section as this can help validate your capabilities and expertise.
- **Publications.** If you have written works that have been published, include a brief description and a URL.

How to Get the Most Out of Your LinkedIn Connections

After you have established your network, it's time to make sure your connections work for you. Here are three helpful tips:

1. **Ask and answer questions.** While you are signed up, you will be able to see a list of questions posted by anyone in your own extended network. Participate in these exchanges to build your reputation and gain more trust. It is also a good idea to ask questions.

2. **Recommend your colleagues.** In LinkedIn, recommendations work as a primary form of currency. Make recommendations for people you have had good experiences with. They will naturally return the favor.

3. **Learn more about your network.** Study the people within your network by reading their profiles. This can be a great

basis for discussion and a foundation to build relationships on.

Google+: Expanding Your Circle

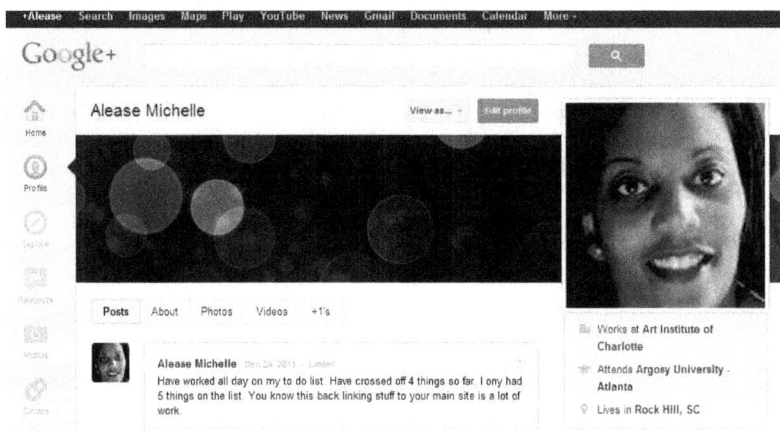

Before its launch, there had been a lot of talks generated by Google+, mostly because it came from Google itself. Since then, it has become an integral part of many social media campaigns.

What is Google+?

Google+ is a social network launched by Google back in July 2011 for limited testing. Users are able to configure and create circles to categorize people they are connected with into different groups as a way of reproducing their real-life relationships. Several months after its launch, Google+ was able to amass 40 million registered users, which is almost one third that of LinkedIn's 135 million members. Despite its growth, it is far from surpassing Facebook, but the figures are certainly not to be ignored.

Why use Google+?

Google+ has a number of cutting edge features, which includes Hangouts, a multi-person video chat. Users can start a Hangout with any of their existing Circles. Another great feature is Sparks, which basically enables a user to locate specific items of interest based on web-based topics. These are all good features, but Google+ also offers…

- **Free traffic boost.** Google+ is built to influence searches for people who you have included in your Circle. This offers a great opportunity to get free promotion from people who like and use the product to people who share your similar interests.
- **Hangouts.** The powerful chat function presents a great opportunity for engaging with other thought leaders in a more personal way. In addition, you can conveniently collaborate and share information and files such as spreadsheets and documents.
- **Distribution of content.** Google+ is a great platform to expand the publication of content distribution. It can be a

great tool for hosts of events and giveaways along with other promotions.

- **Connections with a tech-savvy audience.** People who are in Google+ are the "early adopters" of new technologies, a criterion which presents an ideal target market for many tech savvy people.

- **Targeted audience.** One great advantage of Google+ is the option to share content with specific audiences through Circles. With this feature, you are able to gather data and research on relevant contacts like potential clients and influential personalities in the industry.

Getting Started with Google+

Your Google+ profile will influence the way people perceive you, so make sure you give it as much attention as the other social media platforms you maintain. Listed below are four ways to ensure you get the most from Google+.

1. **Optimize your Page**. As stated, one of the most powerful features of Google+ is the Google search function, so you will want to make sure your page can be easily found with both regular search engines and internal searches. Perform the following:

- **Verify page with Google.** Unlike Twitter that requires a unique handle, there can be a number of pages that may have a similar name to yours. Google has provided a way to verify that the page be the "official" page for a specific brand, which will be given top priority in search rankings.

- **Add a subtitle.** Google+ allows you to place a tag line or subtitle under your brand name, with only the first ten words visible in the header section, and twenty-one characters are shown in pop-ups when users "mouse" over your page. So make sure to keep this in mind when creating your subtitle.

- **Write a compelling introduction.** This is the prime spot on your page, so make sure to use rich keywords that clearly explain who you are and what you do.

2. **Upgrade the visual appeal of your page.** Make the right first impression every time people come to visit your page. You need to grab their attention and interest enough to prompt them to click and add you to their Circles.

- Maximize the creative use of photo editing software

3. **Post with quality content**. Before you even have your first follower, you need to have at least three to four posts since this can help enhance a visitor's first real impression. Perform the following for your posts:
   - Use formatting options to create posts that will look like blog posts.
   - Use videos and photos.

4. **Start attracting followers.** Now that you have optimized your page, you can now open your Google business page for business. Hit the ground running by performing the following:

   - Promote your page using other social media channels
   - Promote your Google page on your website
   - Post content on a regular basis
   - Follow anyone who "Circles" you
   - Create VIP circles and engagers
   - Regularly monitor your comments and streams

RAP EXERCISE

Professionals now collaborate in ways that were unimaginable only a few years ago. They create vast networks, solve complex problems and exchange ideas with colleagues from around the world. To launch and maintain a successful RAP, you have to engage in social media networking. But simply opening an account and updating your profile isn't enough. The time has come that you have to choose at least one social network with which to engage and build community.

1. Choose one social network that was discussed in this action step.

   - Facebook
   - Twitter
   - LinkedIn
   - Google+

2. Explain why you have chosen this platform.

   _____

   _____

   _____

3. Create an account, upload a photo, and fill out your profile.

4. Before inviting friends, populate your page with content for the next few days.

- Create a photo album – upload photos to this album
- Join groups that relate to your interest and industry
- Like pages and update your status

5. Invite friends, family and co-workers to your page. You now have an active page with content, which gives your new fan base something to look through and interact with.

ACTION #8:
SHARE WHAT YOU KNOW
BY BLOGGING

Blogging and social networking are linked in the sense that both contain certain features and certain properties of one another. Both are aimed at creating a wide movement as far as multimedia interaction is concerned. Though it is true that blogs can be regulated and kept private, the main purpose of them is to reach out to a number of people so as to share your reinventing story. The way you go about sharing is similar to this particular function of social networking. The chances of getting an audience at such a platform are high.

Blogging is an ideal way to make new friends and network with more people than you could interact with in the "real" world. Blogging has truly become a platform where various kinds of people from all walks of life, whether they have the same ideologies or not, discuss the matters that are important to them. Blogging now has become an important tool for self- promotion and the selling of products and services online.

I started blogging in 2007. At first I thought blogging was only for people who had something to say or who were natural writers. Blogging has opened a lot of doors for me both personally and professionally. I assist other professionals in the starting of their blogs and I teach a blogging course at the college. Blogging is easy, inexpensive, and profitable and perhaps most importantly, it is fun.

Blogging – Why Niches Matter

Creating a blog is nothing that you need to be afraid of. There is no elaborate planning required either. There are, however, a few things you will need to decide before actually starting a blog. The key aspect of blogging is to determine what you'll be writing about or the nature of the content that you'll be sharing with your readers – this is called niche blogging (narrowing in on a specialized or highly focused topic). Your blog topics can include politics, poetry, arts, current affairs, or almost anything under the sun.

Niche blogging helps boost your RAP. In short, a niche blog makes it easier to market and grow your personal branding image. Here are three good reasons why niche blogs are successful:

1. **Niche blogs create loyal readers.** If you choose a niche, it'll be easier for you to find loyal readers. When people search online, they're often searching for very specific information. If you provide that specific information, they'll likely subscribe to your blog and give you regular access into their lives. This loyalty provides you with an

abundance of opportunities to share what you do and are passionate about.

2. **Niche blogs make money.** Niches are more profitable. By blogging about your specific niche topic, you'll be able to position yourself as an expert. You'll earn the trust of your readers, and as a result, they'll be more likely to buy from you or to trust your recommendations which results in sales. It also means if you are able to draw in a focused audience, you will have a special appeal to targeted advertisers. They know that your audience matches their audience, and they will pay to advertise.

3. **Niche blogs bring in more traffic.** It's easier to compete on the search engines when you have a niche topic. If there's good demand for your topic and you have only a few potential competitors, that means whenever someone searches for your blog topic, they'll find you right away. The result – more traffic.

Before you choose a niche, make sure there are good numbers behind it. That means high demand (lots of people looking for your information) and low supply (not too much competition). When the numbers support it, niches prosper. Choose your niche today and start profiting from your blog.

Choosing a blogging provider

Next, you need to decide which blogging service provider you would like to use. Each blogger provider has its pros and cons. Use the chart below to assist you in making your blogging provider decision.

Blog Platform Comparison Chart

NOTE: *Comparison chart was created based on available information and features are subject to change.*

	Blogger	**WordPress.org**	**TypePad**
Costs	Free	Domain + Hosting, Generally $9 + $5-10/mo (WordPress does not provide web hosting)	$8.95 to $29.95 a Month
Your Own Domain	CMAP Required (Technical)	Yes, default option.	CMAP Required (Technical)
Level of CSS & HTML Required	None	None required for basic functionality, but making any custom edits requires CSS knowledge.	None

	Blogger	WordPress.org	TypePad
Custom Plug-Ins	Limited, through Widgets	Many Highly Functional Plug-Ins	No
Image Storage	1 GB	Depends on Web Host	100 MB for basic, 500 MB for Plus
Customization	Pre-set themes only	HTML, CSS and PHP skills required.	Limited
Software & Security Updates	Automatic	Manual – Forgetting to update can result in a security breach.	Automatic
Ease of Installation	Very easy process	Requires technical knowledge unless you have Fantastico. With Fantastico, setup is 1-click.	Fairly easy, no technical knowledge required *unless* you're mapping a domain name, which can be slightly technical.

Once you have selected your blogging provider and set up your blog, you will notice that it hardly takes fifteen minutes to start publishing content. Maintaining your blog is even easier. Just remember to update frequently, otherwise visitors may stop coming to your blog. Write like you would talk with a close friend as this will keep your content light and interesting. Make sure your content is free of spelling and grammatical errors; this can be a major put-off for many readers.

Where to start?

One of the most challenging things asked of me by my students and clients is: what do I blog about? Although many of them are clear on their niche, they are very unclear on where to start. To make blogging even easier, I've compiled a list of fifty ideas to help get the creative juices flowing.

1. Take a photo. Share a picture instead of words!

2. Share a relevant YouTube video. Perhaps even analyze it a bit in your post. It doesn't require a lot of work to watch and then post and comment on the best videos.

3. Shoot a video of your own. People love to see a blogger's face rather than just read their words.

4. Comment on another blog post on your blog. For example, if another well-known blogger makes a strong statement, respond to that statement on your blog.

5. Comment on a news event and how it relates to your field.

6. Write a "How to" post. Walkthroughs, tutorials and how tos tend to do very well online.

7. Bust a myth. What are common beliefs people hold in your industry that simply aren't true?

8. Tell an entertaining and educational story. What were some turning point moments in your career?

9. Create a Q&A post. What are common questions people have and what are their answers?

10. Examine a Problem. Take an issue that people often get stuck on and go in depth into its causes and solutions.

11. Write a top "x" list. For example, "Top 50 ways to get blog traffic" or "Top 12 hip hop dance moves."

12. Ramble. Just talk aimlessly and passionately about a subject. Be sure to set it aside and read it a day or two later to make sure it's relevant before you post it.

13. Write about common pitfalls. What are mistakes that beginners might make without knowing it?

14. Interview an expert. Post it in audio or video form on your blog.

15. Review a product. What are its benefits and its drawbacks? What sets it apart? Would you recommend it?

16. Comment on the state of the industry. What's going well and what isn't going well?

17. Ask your audience a question. What do they think about topic x?

18. Post the top resources for someone in your industry. Give links, downloads, videos, etc that might help them in what they're trying to do.

19. Make a prediction for the future. What do you think is going to happen in the next twelve months?

20. Write about an in-person event. For example, "What I learned at Affiliate Summit X this year."

21. Share a provocative opinion. What's an opinion you have that just isn't politically correct?

22. Why someone is right or wrong. Write a post about why you think someone is right or wrong about a certain subject.

23. Make something complex simple. Break a hard process down into its parts and make it easy to do or follow.

24. Share a thought process. How do you get from point A to point B in your thought process?

25. Blog about a personal experiment. What's something you tried? Did it work or did it not work? What would you do

differently and what would you recommend?

26. Do an audio recording. Sharing yourself via MP3 rather than text can lead to a stronger connection with your readers.

27. Write a sarcastic post. It shouldn't be aggressive, rather a satirical post that contradicts popular opinion.

28. Give away an eBook. Pack it with value and just give it away for free.

29. Analyze someone else's success. Why did they make it? What did they do differently than other people?

30. Analyze someone else's failure. Why did company X or project X fail? What was the key mistake?

31. Write about an article at the top of Digg or Reddit. These topics are what the movers and shakers online care about right now.

32. Write about the pros and cons of X. What are the benefits and drawbacks?

33. Take the alternate position. What does everyone else think? What do you typically stand for? Try taking the other side.

34. Write about a book that relates to your industry. Review it or write a synopsis.

35. Write a post designed to be inspirational. Not a "how to," but something that gives people a sense that they can do it too.

36. Write an update post – How it used to be, how it is today. For example, "X used to work in the past, but with the recent changes in the market, you really need to do Y to get the same results."

37. Write a post for experts. Give specific how-tos and little known industry knowledge.

38. Write a post for newbies. Make it easy and answer questions that beginners often ask.

39. Share a secret in your industry. What are things that people on the inside know but tend not to share?

40. Do a multi-part post with cliffhangers in between. Write a great post #1, then leave people wanting more before sharing part 2.

41. Write a follow-up on your most popular posts. Take your top three articles and expand on those topics.

42. Host a poll and then post the results. Analyze why you think the poll turned out the way it did.

43. Write an open letter to someone well known in your industry. For example, "An Open Letter to Steve Jobs"

went viral when the iPhone 3GS came out.

44. Show off! What you did and the results you got.

45. A "What I wish I did differently" post. Use what you know now to analyze your successes and failures.

46. Address common frustrations in the industry. Where do people generally get frustrated and not know how to move forward from? Let them know they're not alone.

47. Post an infographic. Take statistics, data and information and put it in graphical form. These tend to get passed around a lot.

48. Around the world view. How is X done similarly or differently around the world?

49. Creative ways to do X. How can you do things differently than other people?

50. How to speed up X. How to do a process faster than it's normally done.

Common Beginner Blogging Mistakes

Ok, I've got you all hyped about blogging, but before you move on to your RAP exercises, I have to share the common beginner blogging mistakes. Not to worry; with this handy list of the most common blogging mistakes, you can avoid them with ease.

- Not being original – Many people are hesitant to be themselves online, yet your personality is what will attract attention and readers. Don't hesitate to be your weird, funky, silly, serious, or controversial self.

- Not giving credit where credit is due – if you borrow information or ideas from anyone, give them the credit. It doesn't weaken your content or your credibility; in fact, it enhances it. And not sourcing your material can get you in a lot of hot water legally.

- Not responding to comments – if you don't want comments, you can set it so people cannot leave them. However, if you want comments, then be sociable and acknowledge them. It helps create a community on your blog. It motivates more comments, and it's just a friendly thing to do.

- Giving up too early – blogs aren't going to achieve instant success overnight. This is why it's so important to enjoy what you're blogging about. Eventually, with enough care and attention, your readership will grow.

- Not posting enough – there's a common rule that says you have to blog every day. You don't have to blog every day. However, if your readers don't hear from you for a week or two, they will forget about you. Keep them happy. Keep them visiting your blog. Publish often.

- Not choosing a topic that you can sustain – if you choose a topic that you're passionate about, you can write every day year around and not lose enthusiasm for your topic. Choose a topic that's not so interesting to you and you'll be lucky to hammer out a blog post a month. It's just not going to work.

- Having too many ads – make sure your blog is content focused. Advertisements are fine. However a blog that's 90% ads and 10% content won't attract a loyal following.

- Forgetting value – people will read your blog because it is: informative, entertaining, or educational. In short, they'll read it because it offers value. Make sure your posts regularly offer value.

- Not promoting your blog – Get out and promote your blog! People won't find you as quickly if you don't shout it from the rooftops. Comment on other blogs and use your blog URL when you register. Participate in social networking and become a guest blogger.

Blogging really is a great way to connect, make a profit and grow a business. Avoid these ten mistakes and you'll achieve blogging success much more quickly and easily. Here's to your blogging success!

RAP EXERCISE

Just like a garden, blogs and social media take time to produce. Focus on quality, not quantity. As a good standard, an investment of thirty minutes twice a week should keep your blog fresh and keep you in touch with readers and comments.

1. Make a list of all the written content (articles, books, case studies, reports, white papers, etc.) you could re-purpose into blog posts.

2. Make another list of topics you would like to write about. Make sure it supports your RAP goals and speaks to your target audience.

3. Now that you have content and topics for your blog, choose a blog provider.

4. Spend a few minutes playing around with posting images, text and maybe videos.

5. Set aside thirty minutes for two days of the week to write and post to your blog.

6. Once you've posted a few articles, share the link to your blog on your social media profile.

ACTION #9:
GET THEM TO CALL YOU

None of the steps we've discussed so far make much difference, of course, if they don't lead to more exposure, clients, job offers or sales. All the social media marketing, goal planning, self-assessments, and blogging: none of it matters if it doesn't lead to something better than what you currently have or are currently doing.

The reason why you plan and create a RAP is to develop stronger relationships. You want people to turn to you as the go-to person every time. That means that people are continually coming back to you, and also sending their friends and acquaintances your way in a steady stream. If planning out a RAP has any value, it's the ability to deliver new relationships on an ongoing basis while maintaining a loyal following. That's how a RAP plan works.

No RAP can possibly be successful if effective follow up measures are not consistently practiced and improved upon. When you meet a new acquaintance, the one that came your way because of your social media engagement, how do you handle this new interaction? Do you move the process along skillfully, or do you assume the new contact is already sold on what you can do? The truth is, when it comes to selling yourself, you can never assume that the deal is done. While your RAP may have done its job of getting you a meeting, the RAP alone can't speak for you. This is the time to ramp up good old fashion selling procedures.

Do you see yourself as a salesperson? Many don't. They often say "Well, I'm just not a salesman." 99% of the people you meet would agree by responding with "I'm not a salesman either." It's easy to dismiss the option of having to sell yourself, but when you make the commitment to reinvent your life, you are also committing to making changes in your life. **So, if this sounds like you, cut it out right now!** The truth is that even if we don't actually have a sales job, you are a sales representative whether you like it or not. And the good news is you can learn how to sell yourself. A willingness to learn how to become great at sales is therefore critical to the successful implementation of your RAP.

When push comes to shove in selling yourself, it helps to know what you are doing. Your RAP helps you create a valuable assessment of yourself, but it's your understanding of sales basics that will have others calling you.

The basics of selling

Be likeable – people are more likely to contact you if you look and sound approachable. This is important in the beginning stages as you only get one chance to make a first impression. To establish likeability:

- Smile. Smiling sends many positive and inviting messages.
- Be "in the moment." When you are preoccupied or distracted, others will feel uncomfortable with you.
- Look others in the eye.
- Ask relevant questions and then listen to the answers without interrupting.
- Provide feedback. This shows you are not only listening, but that you understand and feel that what they are saying is important.

Be credible - a credible person has experience and knowledge. To establish credibility prior to meeting with others, you will need to:

- Explain your achievements and experiences as they relate to your established successes
- Share relevant education. Staying in touch with industry changes shows that you are current with the latest developments.
- Show letters of recommendations or testimonies. The most powerful way to establish credibility is with endorsements from others in your industry.

Be respectful – by respecting others, you ensure that you truly listen to others ideas. In turn, the level of respect you receive from others will increase each time you successfully fulfill a promise. To establish respect:

- Prior to a meeting, send out an agenda that gives an idea of the items you intend to discuss.
- Show up early and avoid lengthy small talk.
- Follow up with the person. Send a thank you note or additional articles/resources that are relevant to the industry and your meeting topics.

These are the basics of selling. I suggest you start small and end big, and remember selling is really nothing more than showing a person how you can help them to live a happier and more successful life.

How to show appreciation

Showing appreciation for others can set you apart from your competitors, increase loyalty, improve retention, inspire sales, and build relationships that last a lifetime. Reaching out to your contacts is also an opportunity to remind them that you exist. Your RAP relies on repeat exposure, and showing appreciation is an affordable and effective way to keep your personal branding in motion.

The following are appreciation strategies that can help you cultivate lasting relationships.

- *Personal thank you notes or greeting cards-* send an unexpected thank you note to a customer following a purchase or whenever a customer has done anything deserving some appreciation. Although sending an email may be quick and easy, you will make a lasting impression by sending a handwritten note in the mail. And as for greeting cards, there are dozens of major and minor holidays throughout the year and each provides a great reason to send a card.

- *Invitations-* spending some time with your top contacts for a special event can also cultivate a relationship that could last a lifetime. Create an event just for them- a special invite to a new showing or to try out a new dessert. If they are geographically dispersed, you can hold a virtual event by inviting them to participate in complementary on-line seminars.

- *Small gifts-* if your budget allows, send flowers, books, a mug full of candy or other token items that make thoughtful gifts for customers. These can be sent on special occasions such as birthdays, holidays, or anniversaries, or can be sent for no reason other than to show your gratitude.

- *The gift of information*- eBooks, reports, workbooks, videos, and other types of informational products can make great gifts. For example, compile a list of useful tips that your friends and acquaintances will appreciate and you can deliver it via-email in a PDF document, print it and give it out, or mail it.

It's important to show appreciation to others. It keeps them coming back to see what you have to offer. Show some love and they will show you the same type of love by purchasing your products or referring others to what you have to offer.

RAP EXERCISE

Now comes the time to practice your basic selling skills. Try selling to a good friend and see what happens. Focus on:

1. Letting your friend share a story.

2. Listening for meaning behind the story.

3. Try to get a deeper understanding of the story. What are the needs and desires?

4. Identify a few solutions to his/her needs and desires.

5. If possible – after the talk – follow up by sending your friend an email referencing additional resources that may assist them even more.

PART 3:
GOING FOR GREATNESS

"Champions aren't made in gyms. Champions are made from something they have deep inside them- a desire, a dream, a vision. They have to have the skill, and the will. But the will must be stronger than the skill."
Muhammad Ali

What is greatness? Well, contrary to what you've been taught, greatness has nothing to do with your profession or with fame. You actually don't have to have won a heavy weight title to be considered great. You can be an artist, a teacher, a mother, or a daughter and still be considered great.

After resigning as department chair in 2005, I was left with a personal evaluation of the work I had done and at the moment, I didn't think the work I had done was great. I actually thought, "What a waste of my time!" I was wrong: it wasn't a waste of time. It was merely the beginning of greatness because the work itself was worthwhile, and this was the only appraisal that counted in the end.

From that moment, I realized that I was an educator who worked in a cubicle. I was no longer an administrator that created and implemented policies and procedures in a corner office. My work wasn't about what I had done for the university - it was about me seeing the value in the work I do. My loyalty would now be directed to the work I do and to the process of doing the work. I've seen the work, I've changed people's lives and businesses, and those changes are what continue to keep me interested in creating great experiences for others.

There are lots of different meanings for greatness, but for our purpose, greatness describes both a person and the first-rate kind of work he or she produces. The one key quality of greatness is the commitment to the process, not just the results. Everyone wants to be great, but not everyone wants to do the work to be great. **Going for Greatness** is about doing, not dreaming. And to be considered great at what you do –you have to self-promote what you do. Self-promotion is essential to the success of your RAP. But how can you do all of this? It takes additional training on un-training the mind to break traditional rules that bind us to the old way of doing things. Breaking rules takes believing in you.

"I am the greatest at what I do." I believe I'm great at what I do, therefore I am great. Do I sound overconfident? Do you think I lack humility for self- promoting my greatness? Understand me, society has too often instilled a sense of self-effacing into our minds. Countless people think of self -promotion as showy and tawdry, and it's the number one reason why they don't do it. But as I have said before, self-promotion is critical to the success of your RAP. Self-promotion, without question, can be challenging and I wish there were a quick- fix solution that I could share with you, but none exists.

However, for the professional who's about doing the work to build and maintain a successful RAP, I can offer you the self-promotion tricks, tips and ideas to help you achieve long-term success.

Part 3- Going for Greatness has been specifically created to help you increase your visibility to make the important connections you need to further your career and improve your professional standing within your industry. The self-promoting ideas in this section are indexed into three action steps: networking, building a website, and public relations (PR). Successful self-promotion is about dedication, hard work, planning and a clear vision of what you want to achieve. In fact, the same promotional strategies discussed in this section are the same ideas that top businesses and executives use daily to win new business and secure clients.

Action # 10
Networking To Create Connections

Why network?

Without question, networking is still the best and easiest way to form long-term relationships with like-minded professionals. It gives you the power of face-to-face relationship building that few other methods of promoting can offer. Additionally, you are building a super powerful alliance that will work tirelessly at promoting you.

Successful professionals understand the power of networking and therefore make an effort to incorporate networking activities into their schedules. They create networking plans so that they know who to reach out to and who may have the biggest impact on their professional development. Networking works and will go a long way to help you reach your RAP goals but only if you take an active role in mastering the art of networking.

Michael Port the author of *Book Yourself Solid* uses the 50/50 networking rule to connect with others. Michael's 50/50 networking rule requires you to not only network with those who might help your career but to also network with other professionals outside of your industry. The 50/50 networking rule will provide you with an opportunity to connect and share what you know and who you know.   If you apply the 50/50 networking rule to your plan, others will begin to notice that you're smart, friendly, and helpful. People will start to like you, enjoy being around you and will remember you when they need someone like you.

Offline and online networking opportunities

The opportunities to network are endless. Anytime you are sharing what you know and who you know with others or learning more about what others do, you're networking. Networking to create genuine connections can take place offline and online; below is a chart explaining simple offline and online networking opportunities.

Offline Networking Opportunities	Online Networking Opportunities
Casual conversation while waiting to be checked out **Attending a workshop or conference** **Becoming involved in community charities or organizations** **Joining a social or sport club**	Business networking websites: LinkedIn.com & Meetup.com Online discussion groups and forums Online membership clubs and learning programs

Attending business and trade association meetings	

What to do at networking events

Create a memorable introduction. Make a memorable impact on people when you introduce yourself. The key to a great introduction is to make it memorable and to instantly tell others what the biggest benefit is of what you do. Your message must be clear, easy to understand and to the point. Here are a few before and after examples:

> **Hair Stylist**
> Before: "I do hair."
> After: "I help people feel and look beautiful."

> **Social Media Consultant**
> Before: "I help solo- entrepreneurs market their products and services online."
> After: "I help solo-entrepreneurs with limited budgets grow their businesses and increase profits."

Have business cards. Business cards are an inexpensive and powerful networking tool when used correctly. Always introduce yourself when handing out your business card and give the other person time to review your card before initiating a conversation. Also get in the habit of handing out at least ten business cards a

141

day- to the postman, store cashier, and even the gas station attendant. You never know where your next referral may come from. Just assume everyone wants to know more about you and what you do.

Donate a door prize. Offering your services as a door prize is another great networking technique that can also be effectively used to generate a ton of interest in what you do. The emcee of the event can do the drawing and announce the winner of your free prize. This small gesture will give the direct exposure you need to be noticed at the event.

Arrive early and stay later. What I've learned is that the best networking opportunities generally take place twenty minutes before the function begins and twenty minutes after the function ends. Greet and speak to as many people as possible before the event and see them off after the end of the event. You will be remembered as the person who was thoughtful enough to take the initiative by greeting them warmly, thus making them feel more comfortable, relaxed and welcomed.

Develop a follow up. After the networking event, take advantage of all of the business cards and personal information you collect while networking by developing a contact list so that you can stay in touch with your new acquaintances. Use an email marketing service like Mailchimp or Constant Contact to build and maintain your list. Get in the habit of following up with new contacts – send them an email, thank you card, newsletter or call them.

Staying in touch with email marketing
Email marketing is quickly becoming a popular form of staying in touch with others. This is because there are many distinct advantages to the concept of email marketing. However, email marketing does have some disadvantages. Let's examine the advantages and disadvantages of email marketing, and I'll also provide some insight into how to plan and execute an effective stay in touch operation.

One of the most significant advantages to email marketing is the ability to reach a large audience with minimal effort. Another major advantage to email marketing is that it's extremely affordable. The costs associated with email marketing are minimal. You can open an account with Mailchimp.com which is free for up to 5,000 subscribers.

The most obvious disadvantage to email marketing is the possibility of having your emails viewed as spam. This is a very important problem because it could prove to be quite a time waster. Emails which contain subject lines or content which appears to be similar to spam may be automatically transferred to a spam email folder by the email system. Emails which aren't automatically deleted may be deleted without being opened simply because the recipient does not recognize the sender of the email. Both of these problems can result in essentially wasted time for you.

Now that you understand the advantages and disadvantages of email marketing, you might wonder how you can maximize email marketing to your advantage. The most important factor to consider is your email distribution list. This list should consist of people who have expressed a desire to receive emails with information from you. The content of the emails should also be carefully considered. They should certainly highlight the great things that are happening with you. Finally, your emails should provide the readers with a call to action. This could be a statement urging the reader to take a specific action such as forward to a friend, or view new videos or photos.

How to get your email subscribers begging for more
Many companies present their promotional materials in a wide variety of methods. Each company has its own distinctive styles and designs, but there is more to it than just a pretty design: the content of your emails must grab and keep the attention of your potential reader. Creativity is the key here, and I've learned a few creative ways to increase email open rates.

- Keep your promotional materials light, creative and original. Many people are stressed out as it is. Getting a stuffy business proposal rather than a lighthearted e-mail may just agitate readers. While you do want your readers to take you seriously, you also want to show them that you know how to have fun.

- Splash some color into your emails as well as provide some photos and articles your reader can relate to. Provide emails that will keep them in a light mood. Make your materials eye catching and grabbing so that they won't be able to take their eyes off of them.

- Have good content, even if it means investing in an experienced and professional copywriter to write them for you. Your content should build trust between you and your readers. It must be informative but not too stuffy. Remove the professional jargon- "talk" to your readers as if they are your closest friends.

- Your promotional materials should be clear. Don't leave people guessing. Explain to them what they need to do in a manner that won't be confusing. Try to anticipate also what your target readers' needs are. Do your research and information gathering before sending out an email.

RAP EXERCISE

Creating a networking plan that creates genuine connections takes work. The prospect of creating a phenomenal network of connections doesn't have to be overwhelming or intimidating. In some form or fashion you are always networking with someone, every day. You now have to do it consciously and with greater awareness until doing it becomes a natural and comfortable part of your daily life. Use the following RAP exercise to help you develop your own personal networking plan.

1. List five books that you believe are "must reads" or that you know contain valuable information that would be of interest to others in your industry and/or outside of your industry. Also write down names of any specific people who come to mind for each book or resource.

Book/Resource   **Person who would be interested**

2. Think of the type of professions that are not represented in your current network. List five that you believe would expand and benefit your network, as well as ideas for where you might find and connect with them.

Professions   **Where to Find them**

3. List three places online and three places offline to cultivate your personal and professional profile while adding value to others.

Online Networking	Offline Networking

Sign up for an Email marketing company. Import email addresses of people who you are interested in staying in contact with then create and send out your first email.

ACTION #11:
YOUR ONLINE OFFICE

After laying out a strong social media marketing foundation, it's time to start thinking about the next important piece of your RAP... the website. In this action step, I'll discuss how the marketing focus of your RAP must work in unison with your website. The purpose of a website is to serve, support, and sell **you**. Whether you are building a website from the ground up, or redesigning an existing site, this action step will shed light on best practices for creating your online office space.

Domain names

In the case of your online presence, your name should be your domain name. That's what people type into their web browser to find your site. I always recommend Domain.com for domain names because their service is exceptional and their pricing is competitive. Of course there are others like: Godaddy.com, Register.com, and Namescheap.com, but for this action step I'm going to stick with what I know and use – which is Domain.com.

To get started, go to http://www.domain.com/, and in the search box in the middle of the page, type the domain name you'd like to buy. Hit "enter" and Domain will tell you if the name you want is available or not, and it will also suggest some alternatives you might be interested in. You may have to try a few different options if you have a common name before you find one that's available.

Some things to keep in mind when choosing a domain:

1. Stick to **.com** domains only – and never purchase the .org or .net (or anything else) when someone already owns the same .com. You'll only lose traffic to the original .com domain.

2. Avoid clever spellings (or deliberate misspellings), numbers, and dashes in your domain name – all this makes your URL hard to share with others.

3. Keep your domain as short as possible – no one wants to type a really long address all the time.

At this stage in the planning process, the most important step is to secure the name you want to build your personal brand around. Once you've found a domain you like, click "add to cart" and then "continue to registration." Then just follow the prompts to set up an account (you'll need this when you set up your hosting account in the next email) and pay for your domain. You can generally ignore all the added features Domain.com will offer along the way, though you might consider paying for several years at a time just so you don't have to worry about renewing your domain every year.

Managing website design and development

Managing website design and development can have endless possibilities. Really good websites can be built using do-it-yourself tools such as Yola.com, Wix.com and Weebly.com. I only suggest building your own website if you're comfortable and handy with technical concepts; otherwise, I suggest you hire a freelance graphic artist and developer from Guru.com or Freelancer.com. There are important components to a successful site, and they should be greatly considered when you start building a website. Building it the right way will ensure you get plenty of traffic – not just today, but repeatedly over time.

What makes a successful website?

A successful website is based on giving real value to your visitors; it should be a website people will actually pass on to their friends because the content is so useful. There's a saying in the world of journalism: "Content is King." It doesn't matter how pretty your site is or how good you are at writing. If the actual content, the real meat of your website, isn't good, then you're not going to attract visitors. Having great content means having your content passed around and getting ranked on Google. If you make sure your content is truly first class, you will then have created a genuine online asset that will pay off in the long run.

Connecting with your visitors is also very important. If you can build a real relationship with the people you're serving, you'll get both links and traffic. You'll also start to become better and more known in your industry. If you treat your industry as just a "target market" to market to, you will get some traffic; however, if you treat your market like you're talking to real people, then you'll actually start to build trust and a reputation in your industry. That's when your site will start moving away from a small-time internet website to a real online office.

What's the difference between a website and a blog?

I get this question a lot from my students and clients. And actually there are no significant differences. In fact, many "websites" are actually using a blogging platform. It's difficult to tell the difference nowadays. But allow me to try to explain a few differences.

Traditional blogging is not so traditional anymore. A traditional blog looked very different from a standard website a few years ago. A traditional blog was simply a chronological series of journal entries. The most recent post is usually displayed first. Today, blogging and blogging technology have grown tremendously. You can have static pages including a static landing page. You can organize your content by category, by tag, and by date. You can also publish video content on your blog, sell products or services and essentially accomplish anything on a blog that you can on a website.

That being said, websites may be more useful if you're building a site around a concept or information. With a blog, there is still the fact that the content is dated. People come to expect frequent posts. With a website, you can publish new content whenever it fits your purposes. There isn't the same expectation for new content.

BLOG

Simple Marketing Tactics that Increase Sales

Posted on May 29, 2013

For many new entrepreneurs marketing can be extremely complex or quite simple. Ironically, the simple marketing tactics are the ones that are most effective and successful. Value-added headlines, informative content, and visual appeal are simple marketing tactics that can increase your business's bottom line.

For example, one simple tactic is to make it quick and easy for web visitors and customers to view information on your website. Allowing adequate white space, creating short sentences, and keeping enough space between words, sentences, and paragraphs will make your site more appealing.

RECENT POSTS
- Simple Marketing Tactics that Increase Sales
- Put Online Marketing to Work for Your Business
- 5 Ways to Create Income With Your Blog

RESOURCES
- Alease Michelle
- School of Creative Business

WEBSITE

Home   About Me   Artwork   Blogs   Others Say...   Media   Contact

alease michelle

Educator. Artist. Creative Director. Consultant. Motivational Speaker. Entrepreneur

Testimonial

" This piece is an exquisitely unique and capsulated view of my 30+ year journey of membership and leadership in Sigma Gamma Rho Sorority Inc. Every time I look at it, a flood of memories is regenerated that makes me smile and more appreciate

Usability differences. Traditionally blogs are much easier for an online beginner to use and maintain. In fact, you can maintain your blog from your smart phone or tablet. However, website building technology has become easier too. If you're comfortable adding plug-ins and modifying the code on a blog, you'll be comfortable modifying or creating the code for a website too.

The cost. One of the biggest differences between a blog and a website may be cost. A WordPress blog or website is practically free. You'll pay for your domain name, for your hosting, and a small $10 fee to WordPress.org. There are literally thousands of free templates that you can upload and customize yourself. You can also purchase a customizable template. Website templates can also be customized and you can find many for free, but the customization is often very limited. And if you want a template that offers more features, it can get expensive.

Purpose driven decisions. Before you decide whether to blog or create a website, consider the purpose for your online presence. If you are interested in showcasing who you are and what you do, then a website may be your best choice. If you are creating a content rich information site or if you are selling a service, then a blog can be a better choice. Determine your needs, goals and purposes first. Then compare blogging options versus traditional website options. The answer may be much easier to determine once you know exactly what you need your site to accomplish.

Website traffic tips

It's time to explain how to get traffic to your online office. The reality is that it isn't as hard as you think. It does take work, but it's not difficult work. Here are several proven traffic sources and methods I've used to consistently bring people to my sites.

- Create a site with valuable content, products or services.

- Research and use Google search words in your content. Find actual search terms people enter into Google when conducting a search. This will help you achieve better rankings.

- Place keywords within the first twenty-five words in your page content and spread them evenly throughout the document.

- Use your keywords in your blog post title, website page names, photo names and descriptions.

- Keep your site design simple so that your customers can navigate easily between web pages.

- Submit your web pages, i.e. every web page and not just the home page, to the most popular search engines and directory services. Hire someone to do this for you if you are unsure of how this works.

- Monitor your competitors and the top ranked websites to see what they are doing right in the way of design, navigation, content, keywords, etc.

- Make your customers' visits easy and give them plenty of ways to remember you in the form of newsletters or free reports

- Demonstrate your industry and product or service expertise by writing and submitting articles to other blog sites so you can continue to be perceived as an expert in your field.

- When not sure, hire professionals. It may seem costly, but it is a lot less expensive than spending your money on a website which no one visits.

- Don't look at your website as a static brochure. Treat it as a dynamic, ever-changing sales tool and location.

- Pictures are worth a thousand words. Studies have shown that websites that are illustrated are more trusted and visited than sites that aren't.

RAP EXERCISE

It is very unlikely you'll find a successful professional without a web presence. It's a critical aspect of reinventing yourself. If you don't have some kind of web presence (online office) you are missing out on the best and most efficient way to start a conversation about what you do. The following RAP exercise will get you started with building your online office.

1. What's the primary objective of your website?

   _____

   _____

2. Locate two websites you like. List what you like and
   dislike about them. Is the site a blog, website or both? Can
   you identify what platform they used to build the site?

   (Hint: Scroll down to the bottom of the site.)

Website Name	Likes/Dislikes	Blog/Website/ Both	Website Platform

3. Do a little research on website platforms. Weebly.com,
   Yola.com and Wix.com are good DIY website builder sites.
   Then make the decision to either hire a professional web
   designer or create the website yourself.

Action #12:
The Ultimate Self-Promotion Strategy

The ultimate self- promotion strategy for a successful RAP is to incorporate public relations or simply "PR" into your action plan. No other marketing method delivers so much impact for so little investment of time and money. The public values media opinion and so should you. Good and strategic media exposure will help you establish a reputation and personal brand that will reach far more prospects than you could imagine. Getting media attention will require some effort on your part. The strategies discussed in this action are designed to enhance your RAP and are quite easy when you take the time to understand and follow a few simple guidelines.

The benefits of media exposure

Unlike advertising, PR is about obtaining favorable media mentions about you and what you do for free. Although it requires hard work, it's the most cost-effective way to reach your desired audience. Here are the kinds of results you can expect:

Immediate credibility. The more often someone sees your name, the more predisposed they are to you and what you are passionate about. It implies you are competent and sought after for your wisdom.

Increased reach. No matter how much you network online and offline, you can only get so far on your own. PR quickly exposes you to a larger audience, sometimes even national attention.

Enhance reputation. When your name appears in print or is mentioned live on TV or radio, you've acquired an aura of expertise that will get you more prestige. Any media coverage you obtain can be used long afterwards- reprints of articles and taped recordings can make excellent marketing materials that are more convincing than anything you could create yourself.

Integrating PR into your RAP

You will need to craft a PR plan that's consistent with your RAP and your audience. If you have followed the previous action steps, which I know you have, then you have an established foundation from which to launch your PR plan. Because PR is central to the success of your RAP and self-promotion strategy, PR needs to be an integral part of your everyday planning process. Integrating PR into your RAP requires that you:

- Read everything relating to your industry.
- Identify media sources that reach your target audience.
- Attend trade shows, seminars and other events related to your industry.

- Build a media list, which will be composed of media outlets and media personnel to whom you will send your "news".
- Write press releases, fact sheets, and pitch letters.
- Brainstorm ideas on how you can turn your RAP message into newsworthy information.
- Write articles and be interviewed.
- Pitch your story.

Press releases

A press release can be considered the main tool used to secure media attention, and it's one that is easy to create regardless of your experience. The following information will give you the basics in terms of format, style and design of what's required to create a press release. Each press release should include the following:

FOR IMMEDIATE RELEASE:	These words should appear at the top left of the page, in upper case. If you don't want the story to be made public yet, write "HOLD FOR RELEASE UNTIL ...." instead.
Headline	Just like a headline in a newspaper. Make sure this describes the content in your story.

City, State/ **Month** **Day, Year**	These details answers the where and when.
Body	This is where the actual story is placed. There should be around two paragraphs, each paragraph no more than three to four sentences. If there is more than one page, write "-more-" at the bottom of the page.
Bio Information	Include any background information about yourself.
Contact **Information**	Include contact person, company name, phone/fax, email, & address.
ENDS or ###	This indicates the end of the press release.
(xxx words)	If you like, you could include the total number of words contained in the press release.

Press release example

Contact:
Alease McClenningham

PO Box 36013
Rock Hill, SC 29732
803- 487-7873
designsbyalease@yahoo.com

For Immediate Release
December 21, 2009

Press Release

Work by African American Mixed Media Artist, "Alease Michelle" McClenningham, Selected for Somerset Studio Gallery Winter 2010 Issue

Rock Hill, SC, - debuting in 1997 from Laguna Hill, CA, Somerset Studio has become a leading publication within the art and crafting industry. Somerset Studio is a bimonthly magazine which attracts a large and devoted following of readers seeking the latest innovations in the art of paper and mixed-media. Somerset Studio publishes a gallery issue biannually which includes hundreds of samples of extraordinary artwork presented up close and in detail for mixed media artist around the country.

Mixed Media Artist "Alease Michelle" McClenningham's works, *My Sister's Keeper*, *Innocence*, and *Sista* - were selected as part of Somerset Studio Gallery Winter 2010 issue. Alease Michelle has been creating mixed media art in her home studio for the past 5 years. Her mixed media collages include images of African American women and men dating back to the 1920s. Alease Michelle's mixed media collages have been displayed in several galleries in the Carolinas. She has lectured on the creative process of her visual storytelling style and has demonstrated many of her techniques at art colleges and artist guilds.

Alease Michelle holds a BA in Art Studio from the University of South Carolina, an MA in Visual Arts from Goddard College in Plainfield, VT, and is currently working toward a doctoral degree in Education from Argosy University in Atlanta, GA. For the past 11 years, Alease Michelle has been a college instructor in the fashion and management department at The Art Institute of Charlotte.

##

Once you have written and proofread your press release, you are ready to send it out. The good news is the Internet has changed the way publicists and the media send and receive news information.

Guess what? You can take full advantage of this by distributing your press releases electronically. Although there are still a few editors who still like press releases mailed or faxed to them, you will find that many of them are jumping aboard the electronic submissions train. Most media directories in print or online will ask for email contact information. If you locate a company that doesn't ask for email contact information, just assume they would rather have the press release mailed or faxed. Below is a list of sites you can submit your press release to electronically. On a side note: submitting your press release electronically will increase traffic to your online office.

www.Free-Press-Release.com

www.webwire.com

www.24-7pressrelease.com

www.PressReleaseSpider.com

Pitching your story

Pitching your story to the media begins with seeing your story from the media's perspective. Only when you learn to align your story with the media's interest will the media want to write and quote you. There are plenty of ways to prove to the media that you deserve their coverage, but all will ask, 'What makes this news worthy?"

If you are wondering what you should write about, consider these ideas on what makes your story news worthy:

1. Starting a new business
2. Introduction of a new product
3. Celebrating an anniversary
4. Writing a book
5. Receiving an award
6. Participating in a charity event
7. Introducing a new strategy or idea
8. Publishing a statement on a position regarding a local, regional, or national issue
9. Launching a website or blog
10. Announcing that you're available to speak on particular subjects of interest
11. Announcing you've reached a major milestone
12. Obtaining a new, significant client

13. Sponsoring a workshop or seminar

14. Making public statements about trends within your industry

15. Forming a new strategic partnership or alliance

Deciding on what is news worthy is easy, right? I hope the list helps. Next is crafting the pitch letter. The pitch letter is exactly that: a letter that you write to explain the reason why you should be featured in print or on air. Pitch letters are short and to the point- a lot more informal than a press release. Use the pitch letter as a way to convince the editor, journalist or producer that your story idea is a good one. It will serve as a tool to open the door and the line of communication between you and the media.

Additionally, I recommend you send support documents with your pitch letter – like a fact sheet (insights about you in bullet point form), photographs, or even product samples – basically anything that you feel will help to support your story.

Never stop promoting

One of the greatest myths about success is that eventually you will be totally embraced by the masses. Creating a successful RAP isn't a build it and they will come action plan. Your RAP is about build it and never stop promoting it, and the masses will eventually come and keep coming as long as you never stop promoting the wonderful things you do.

Successful professionals know the power of promotion and when promotion stops or slows, so does public awareness of what you want to be known for. Because of this, the world's most successful people have learned to become publicity hounds.

Are you wondering how do you keep the self-promotion efforts going? It's stress-free when you know the secrets.

Secret #1- Become an expert media source. Become a member of ExpertClick.com. and HARO.com The purpose of these directories is to give members of the media quick and easy access to experts who can assist them and supply information they need to complete a story.

Secret #2 – Start a PR idea folder. One of the easiest ways to get ideas is to simply gather information from other people's outstanding publicity and news making ideas. Every time you see, hear, or read a great news making idea, write it down, print/cut it out and put it in your PR ideas folder.

Secret #3 – Think photo opportunity. Print and television media love a good photo opportunity and often it's much easier to create one than to create a good news story. You can contact the media by way of a press release, pitch letter or phone call. Or you can even take the photograph yourself and send it to the newspaper, magazine or online publication along with a paragraph or two explaining the details. Use the "pitching your story list" for ideas which might make for a great photo opportunity.

Secret #4 – Create an offering of goodwill. Although the spirit of giving is great, you also want to make sure that you will get something in return for your kind gesture. Promote what you do within your local community by donating your resources, services or offering discounts and invite the media to attend.

Secret #5 – Write letters to the editors. Along with writing and sending press releases, you can also write letters to the editor of a newspaper, magazine, or trade journal. Just remember your letters have to be more than a simple advertisement promoting what you do. Try to tie your letter into a local hot topic, or position yourself as someone with expert information on the topic.

Secret #6 – Create a PR page on your website. On your PR page, include a downloadable media kit. Your media kit will contain your summary sheet (similar to a table of contents, it allows the reader to quickly decipher what's in your media kit), current and past press releases, fact sheet, bio sheet, testimonials/ recommendations, photos of you and media clippings.

RAP EXERCISE

I strongly believe that every professional should implement an ongoing public relation campaign. There are very few forms of advertisement that can match the effectiveness and credibility of free publicity. We all take in some type of media exposure into our daily lives. Whether it's watching television, listening to the radio, or surfing the internet, we do so because we want to be informed and entertained. Great media exposure can have the same impact on your target audience; it will serve you well as you journey into greatness.

1. List 4 pitchable story ideas.

Pitchable Story Ideas
1.
2.
3.
4.

2. Choose one idea and write your first press release.

3. Submit your press release to 2 online PR directories.

4. Upload your press release to your blog or website.

5. Send your press release to your email list.

LAST ACTION:
THE EXHORTATION

"Keep away from people who try to belittle your ambitions. Small people always do that, but the really great make you feel you, too, can become great." **Mark Twain**

There's one last action step, I need to share with you. I don't think what I've said in this book is that shocking or different. In fact, I think most of what I've shared is very simple and practical. Actually, I'm committed to sharing it because I want to be part of the dramatic shift in consciousness I feel is going to take place in your life. I want to be part of the change you experience from self-doubt and averageness to happiness and sustainable success.

As you move forward to launching into the next level of success in your life, I encourage you to consider one last action step. Just as a boxer must stretch and warm up his body before a fight, you need to warm up your entrance into a new area of growth, productivity, and fulfillment. In fact, this last action step that I'm going to recommend to you is one that many successful professionals utilize on a daily basis.

What is this action step? See it's really easy: successful professionals often envision themselves going through the sophisticated motions of their most exceptional performances. From beginning to end, they mentally visualize each detail that will happen next; it's like watching a movie about yourself.

Many people know all of the information that I have presented in this book, but they still struggle with taking action. They've done the due diligence of reading each action step and have actually executed the RAP exercises, yet they often experience fear and self-doubt. What's missing is often the ability to see themselves achieving true greatness. You have to be willing to trust your gut, and take the necessary risk of putting yourself out there. Understand this: I know it can be tempting to paralyze yourself because of the possibilities. But as you have read from my experiences, waiting for others to validate you and your decisions or to make the decision for you isn't good; as a matter of fact, it's suicide. From doing what you have to do, to making sure you do what you want to do: both are **CHOICES**.

After you have read all of the action steps, participated in all of the RAP exercises, you must not be afraid to visualize and proceed. In the book, *Secrets of the Millionaire Mind*, T. Harv Eker quoted Marianne Williamson in her book, *A Return to Love*. She says it best:

You are a child of God. Your playing small does not serve the world. There is nothing enlightened about shrinking so that other people won't feel insecure around you. We are all meant to shine, as children do. We were born to make manifest the glory of God that is within us. It is not just in some of us, it is in everyone. And as we let our own light shine, we unconsciously give other people permission to do the same. As we are liberated from our own fear, our presence automatically liberates others.

Take the steps, one after another, to bring your best self forward. Whether you end up taking action or not, the one thing I know that's right- you are a child of God and He wants you to be **GREAT!** Remember *Greatness is in the Comeback*!

May you live long and prosper.

Love,

Aleane

APPENDIX

"Stop being afraid of what could go wrong and start being positive about what could go right." **George Clooney**

A Personal Branding Crash Course.

Let's wrap up with a quick overview of the primary steps you should commit to ensure your RAP is achievable and successful.

Step #1. Create a workable schedule. Until you get a clear idea of your work and non-work habits, you may never have the proper motivation to complete your RAP. Create a schedule that includes your daily and weekly activities and don't forget to schedule in some "me time".

Step #2. Your story. In 4 to 6 sentences, write out a short verbal explanation of who you are, what your vision is, and why you care.

Step#3. Social media marketing plan. Write out your social media marketing goals. Open an account on 1 social media platform. Create content to share and engage in genuine conversations with others online.

Step#4. Email marketing. Create your first email marketing campaign. Send out a monthly email to your contact list. Provide quality content that can be shared with others.

Step#5. Build an online office. Design your website or hire a professional. Make sure your online office is easy to navigate through and provides quality and sharable content.

Step #6. Promotion plan. Write and send out a press release on a special event you are hosting or a special award you've received.

At this point what I should really do is suggest that you go back through the RAP exercises one more time, but I know that would take more of your time when actually it's time to take action. Let me also warn you that you can't wait until everything is perfect before you send out anything. If you were to implement just 10% of what I've presented in this book, you would be 300% ahead of where you were yesterday and 100% ahead of other professionals who are waiting on someone else to validate them. Let this be the day you do one thing that moves you in the direction of becoming **GREAT!**

Additional Reading and Resources

BOOKS

Personal Development

Before You Do: Making Great Decisions That You Won't Regret by T.D. Jakes

The Vision Board by Joyce Schwarz

In the Meantime: Finding Yourself and the Love You Want by Iyanla Vanzant

Sun Stand Still: What Happens When You Dare to Ask God for the Impossible by Steven Furtick

Lifetime Plan for Success: Great Bestselling Works Complete In One Volume by Dale Carenegie

It's Your Time: Activate Your Faith, Achieve Your Dreams, and Increase in God's Favor by Joel Osteen

The Alchemist by Paulo Coelho

Style Statement: Live by Your Own Design by Danielle LaPorte and Carrie McCarthy

Business

The Complete Idiot's Guide to Branding Yourself by Sherry Beck Paprocki and Ray Paprocki

**The 4 hour Work Week: Escape 9-5, Live Anywhere, and Join the New

Rich by Timothy Ferriss

Become Your Own Boss in 12 months: A Month-by-Month Guide to a Business that Works by Melinda Emerson and Michael C. Critelli

The Girl's Guide to Starting Your Own Business: Candid Advice, Frank Talk, and True Stories for the Successful Entrepreneur by Caitlin Friedman and Kimberly Yorio

The Purple Cow: Transform Your Business by Being Remarkable by Seth Godin

The Referral Engine: Teaching Your Business to Market Itself by John Jantsch

The Automatic Millionaire: A Powerful One-Step Plan to Live and Finish Rich by David Bach

Think and Grow Rich by Napoleon Hill

Social Media

Customer Service: New Rules for Social Media World by Peter Shankman

301 Ways to Use Social Media to Boost Your Marketing by Catherine Parker

The New Relationship Marketing by Mari Smith

Social Media Marketing an Hour a Day by Evans and Bratton

30 Days to Social Media Success: The 30 Day Results Guide to Making the Most of Twitter, Blogging, LinkedIN, and Facebook by Gail Martin

ProBlogger: Secrets for Blogging Your Way to a Six-Figure Income by

Darren Rowse

Kindle Downloads

Achieve Anything in Just One Year: Be Inspired Daily to Live Your Dreams and Accomplish Your Goals by Jason Harvey

Have it Your Way by Nicholas Bate

Transform Your Life by Penny Ferguson

Facebook Fame: The Facebook Marketing Bible For The Small Business by Laura Roeder

WEBSITES

Self- Management & Promotion

Contact me.com - organize and keep track of all contacts and leads

Re.vu – instead of sending a resume, create a story about yourself

Formsite.com– build professional online html forms and web surveys

Entrepreneur.com/formnet – access to hundreds of business forms, templates and contracts

PR in a box.ca – online public relations kit

Mailvu.com – send video emails to anyone using your web cam

Faxzaero.com – send an online fax for free

Content Management

Scribd.com – documents and books at your fingertips! Read, print, download and send

Socialoomph.com – increase your online productivity

Hello bar.com – direct your visitors and promote your most important web content

Myblogguest.com – community of guest bloggers

Storify.com – tell stories by curating social media content

Lovely charts.com – create flowcharts, network diagrams, and sitemaps

Nutshellmail.com – get your Facebook and Twitter streams in one location in your inbox

Bagtheweb.com – helps users curate web content for any topic to collect, publish, and share

Alertful.com – quickly setup email reminders for important events

Google.com/dictionary – get word meanings, pronunciation and usage examples

Polishmywriting.com – check your writing for spelling and grammatical errors

Video and Photos

Vidcaster.com – create a video library

Screencast-o-matic.com – online screen recorder for one click recording from your browser

Free digital photos.net – download free images for use in corporate and personal projects

Photoscape.com – easy photo editing software that enables you to fix and enhance photos

Freescreensharing.com – unlimited Free webinar meetings

Sumopaint.com – an excellent online image editor

Stupeflix.com- make a movie out of your image, audio, and video clips

Sxc.hu – download stock images absolutely free

BLANK WORKABLE SCHEDULE

TIME/DAY	MONDAY	TUESADAY	WEDNESDAY	THURSDAY	FRIDAY	WEEKENDS
7:00 am						

BONUS OFFER

GREATNESS IS IN THE COMEBACK
A Poetic Soundtrack that's inspiring and energizing.

featuring,

2010 Emmy Award Winning,
2010 Southern Fried Poetry Slam,
13th Ranked in the Internationally
Individual World Poetry Competition
Slam Master, Boris "Bluz" Rogers
&
Music Producer,
One Son Entertainment

FREE DOWNLOAD
http://aleasemichellestudio.com/the-comeback-soundtrack/

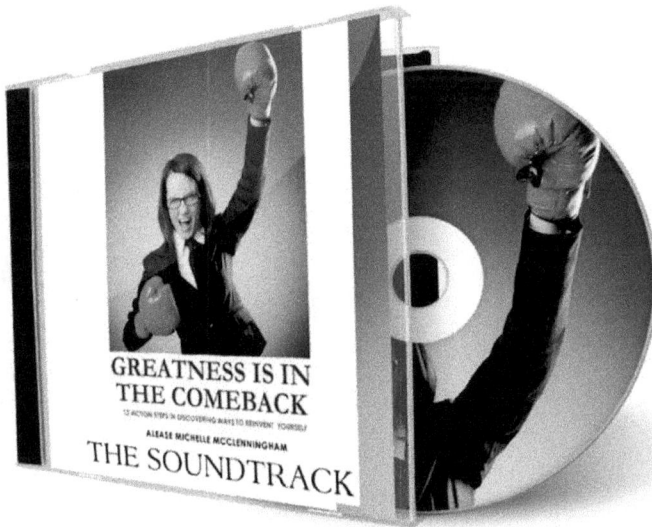

ABOUT THE AUTHOR

Educator, Expert & Artist. As the owner of Alease Michelle Studios, LLC and the editor of the School of Creative Business, "Alease Michelle" McClenningham combines fourteen years of teaching experience and an established artistic career with a powerful interest in online branding and marketing. Her desire is to empower others to create new, unique, and sustainable lifestyles—and to enjoy doing it!

Alease holds a B.A. in Art Studio/Graphic Design from the University of South Carolina, and an M.A. in Visual Arts from Goddard College. She is a member of Sigma Gamma Rho Sorority, Inc., York County Arts and Science Council, Toastmasters International, Association of Strategic Marketing and the Association of Professional Women.

As an expert, Alease lends knowledge to the press, editorials, and serves as a subject-matter expert. She is a sought-after presenter on the topics of creative marketing and management, personal image and branding, and fashion related topics. As a creative entrepreneur, her adventurous spirit has led to fashion show production, wardrobe consulting, and visual merchandising.

She serves as an Associate Professor at an art and design college in Charlotte, NC and teaches a wide range of courses in Fashion Marketing and Management. She serves on several committees and organizations, and works to improve curriculum and processes that have produced quantifiable results.

Alease has risen to the challenge of teaching others how to blend their passion with today's technology to run a successful business. She helps creative entrepreneurs produce powerful products and services that resonate with their target audience, develop a persuasive sales message, and position themselves as experts in their niche.

You can personal connect with Alease on her website www.aleasemichelle.com and you can also connect with Alease on the following social web places:

Facebook: www.facebook.com/AleaseMichelle www.facebook.com/greatnessisinthecomeback

Twitter: www.twitter.com/AleaseMichelle

Youtube: www.Youtube.com/Aleasetv

LinkedIn: www.linkedin.com/in/AleaseMichelle